Praise for

"Dwier Brown is a great storyteller—I couldn't put his book down! He entertains us with behind-the-scenes stories about *Field of Dreams*. He moves us with stories about his own father and the fathers of countless strangers who have approached him because of his role in the movie. He delights us with colorful tales of growing up in rural Ohio and overcoming his inherited stoicism to become an actor. If you loved *Field of Dreams*, or if you just love your father—or wish you could—you'll love this book."
  – Lawrence Kessenich, editor of *Shoeless Joe,* the basis for *Field of Dreams*

"For Dwier Brown, who played Kevin Costner's father in *Field of Dreams*, it was the scene of a lifetime. For fans, it was a powerful, evocative game of catch that still resonates 25 years later. Many actors may have bigger names, but few could write as artfully about their craft. Read this book, and you'll know much more about the movie, the meaning and the man behind the magic."

-New York Times

"It's no surprise that Dwier Brown beautifully captures what it was like to film the ending of *Field of Dreams* - after all, he is the ending. What is a revelation is the deeply emotional and honest telling of his story, and - just like the movie - of a father-son relationship you won't forget."
  - Phil Robinson, writer/director of *Field of Dreams*

"The book is amazing. With *If You Build It...*, Brown makes a powerful literary statement of his own, and reminds us again about the magical, complicated, and lasting bond between fathers and sons. It is a personal journey you won't want to miss."

-New York Daily News

More praise for *If You Build It...*

"Dwier Brown has written a wonderfully funny and unforgettably charming memoir. He makes a poetic and convincing case that he was somehow fated, if not born, to play the role of John Kinsella, and in his book he has chronicled America's love for baseball and for a movie that touches the heart of anyone who's ever missed his dad."

— Rick Cleveland, Emmy-winning writer and producer
The West Wing, Six Feet Under and House Of Cards

"Dwier Brown is a master story-teller, writing from his heart and awakening yours."

— Marianne Williamson, author of *A Return To Love*

"Dwier Brown's *If You Build It...* is, on the surface, about five unforgettable moments in a cornfield in the movie *Field of Dreams*. But it is much more about baseball and dreams and overcoming disappointments and fathers. When I finished it. I wanted to call my Dad and say, "Wanna play catch?""

— Joe Posnanski, NBC Sports, former writer at *Sports Illustrated*, twice voted best sports columnist in America by the Associated Press Sports Editors

"Dwier Brown has written a wonderful book. He's managed to elicit much of the same pathos of the movie. He's deftly woven the narrative of the film's creation, the narrative of his career, the evolution of his relationship with his father, and the extrapolation of all of our relationships with our fathers and sons. I absolutely LOVE all of the interludes. Not only are they examples of some of his best writing, but wow, every one of them brought tears to my eyes."

— Brad Herzog, *Why Not Books*

More praise for *If You Build It...*

"Wow. I can't ever remember reading any book that was such a beautiful combination of warm stories, humor, personal reflection, intimate sharing, honesty and vulnerability, gentleness and insight... it is a major accomplishment, and a wonderful and inspiring contribution on many levels. I was touched and moved over and over again. I feel inspired by it."
                                                    - David Feigin, producer

"I have to give author Dwier Brown a lot of credit. His honest story telling invites you in like an old friend, and his relationships – those with his father, his mother, even stars of the movie – feel like my own. I encourage anyone who's a fan of the movie or looking to explore their relationship with their own father to give this one a read. You'll finish the book in one sitting, whether that was your intention or not."
                                                    -*Post Newspapers*

"The book is the journey of a struggling actor, that transparently, and humbly walks us through his fascinating life. I'm not saying I couldn't put it down, I'm saying I never wanted to put it down. Brown is as gifted a writer as you will find, and the non-fiction tale he writes will have something for everyone. As a dad, you will re-think parenting, as a writer you will re-think writing. The book should be a number one best-selling book on Amazon, or anywhere else. I will be gifting this book and recommending it to everyone. READ THIS BOOK!"
                                    - Stephen Costello, award-winning author
                                    and Vice-President of Steiner Sports

"I don't like the book. I don't love it. I ADORE it! I'm afraid when I plunge in, I'll keep reading and miss our game! It is written in such a wonderful voice, with such an audible style. So lyrical. It has a gentle velocity to it. It moves so well. And it is SO moving."
- Dr. Charles Steinberg, Executive Vice-President of the Boston Red Sox

IF YOU BUILD IT...

DWIER BROWN

Copyright © 2014 by Dwier Brown

All rights reserved. In accordance with the U.S. Copyright Act of 1976,
the scanning, uploading, and electronic sharing of any part of this book
without the permission of the publisher constitute unlawful piracy
and theft of the author's intellectual property. If you would like to use
material from the book (other than for review purposes), prior written
permission must be obtained by contacting the publisher at Elsie Jean
Books, P.O. Box 964, Ojai, CA, 93024.
Thank you for your support of the author's rights.

Some names and identifying details have been changed to
protect the privacy of individuals.

ISBN 978-0-9960571-0-3
First Edition: April 2014, Second Edition: 2015

Published in the United States by
Elsie Jean Books
P.O. Box 964, Ojai, CA, 93024
www.dwierbrown.com

Cover photo by Melinda Sue Gordon, courtesy of Universal Studios
Printed in the United States of America

For My Parents

Walter Warren Brown
(March 7, 1921 – June 13, 1988)

and

Elsie Jean Ferris Brown
(November 5, 1922)

If You Build It . . .

LIVING AND DYING IN L.A.

"There are only two ways to live your life.
One is as though nothing is a miracle. The other is as if everything is."
- Albert Einstein

In the fall of 1986, I was desperate. My acting career was at a stand-still. I had spent a year and a half doing plays in Chicago, and I hit the ground in Los Angeles at a full run in 1981. I had played Stuie, one of the Cleary sons, in the acclaimed miniseries the *Thorn Birds* and a doctor in *To Live and Die in L.A.*, helmed by Academy Award-winning director William Friedkin. I had done a succession of guest star roles on television, but I felt like I was dying.

The feeling had some basis in reality: In the previous five years I had been killed over a dozen times. In films and on TV, I had been shot to death six times, died of a heart attack, been lynched, and knifed and, in the *Thorn Birds*, run over by a wild pig (which I affectionately called being "boared to death"). On stage, I had been stabbed, died of old age and, in an amazing *tour de force* of death, had my neck broken *and* died of an aneurism in the same play.

If expiring repeatedly in various roles wasn't a metaphor for my dying career, I don't know what was. Having had some success in my first few years in Hollywood, I was disillusioned by how empty "success" felt and how most of the shows I was dying in weren't changing the world the way I had imagined they would when I left my family's farm to become an actor six years earlier.

So, on Halloween night in 1986, I made a deal with God. As I was getting ready to go to a costume party dressed as my favorite movie star, Jimmy Stewart, I looked in the full-length mirror. There I was, dressed in an old-fashioned football jersey. I turned to look at the paused, flickering image of Mr. Stewart on my VCR from the "I'd lasso the moon" scene and I took stock. It seemed hopeless. In that dark, desperate moment of despair, I told God that if He would put me in just one "meaningful" film like *It's A Wonderful Life*, I would try to use that opportunity to help people.

I had come to love Frank Capra's classic 1946 film about the suicidal George Bailey, who magically gets to see what the world would be like without him and finally realizes his value. As a kid, I knew the movie was corny but, as I got older, I realized what a gift it would be to see the difference we each make in the lives of others.

I wanted to use what I had learned becoming an actor to help people and I wanted the film industry to make movies that could make that happen. In short, I wanted to change the world. So on a dark Halloween night in my apartment in Hollywood I made that deal with God. But like many people who make such deals, after the panic passed, I forgot all about it.

I didn't know then that subtle forces were at work to make my dream come true. I would be given the chance to be in a movie that would change people's lives, but I would have to be ready for it to change my life, too. For once, I wouldn't have to play a character who dies at the end of the movie, I would have to play one who is dead before the movie even starts.

GREEN ACRES

"Green acres is the place for me.
Farm livin' is the life for me.
Land spreadin' out so far and wide…"
- *Green Acres* TV show theme song, by Vic Mizzy

When I was eight years old, in the middle of my fourth grade year, my fa ther got the idea that he should move his family from the comfort of our suburban duplex to a farm in the middle of nowhere.

The house he found was a hulking two-story affair in Sharon Center, Ohio. It had been built in 1818 and had been struck by lightning sometime in the 1930's, causing the roof to be partially burned off. Although the charred roof had been covered over, there were no indoor toilets and the house was in such a state of disrepair that the farmer who was selling the 52 acres on which it stood was willing to throw in the house for *free*.

It seemed like a great deal to my father, who had been forced to abandon his dream of becoming a doctor and given up his dream of corporate success, but still had his dream of remodeling an old house. Even though the house was free, my mother, sister, brother and I were sure Dad was getting taken. But we moved in anyway.

On the slushy, January morning of my ninth birthday, after I got up for school and walked through the drizzle and melting snow to go to the bathroom in our corrugated iron outhouse (there was *still* no indoor toilet), I found myself standing on a makeshift ladder leading down to our new, dirt basement (there were no stairs), passing buckets of muddy meltwater to my siblings who would, in turn, pass them on to my mother who would toss them onto the pile of dirty, melting slush in our side yard.

Back and forth we passed the buckets as my father cheerfully yelled "Bucket brigade!" from his position in freezing, calf-deep mudwater in the shallow basement, hoping to fool us into thinking that this emergency morning flood was some kind of an impromptu dawn submarine game, and not a preview of our new life on *Green Acres*. No one was fooled.

For the next twelve years, until I moved to Chicago to become an actor, my brother and sister and I tore down lath and plaster walls and built new ones with drywall, moved every door in the house to a different location, dug the entire basement four feet deeper, by hand with a pick and shovel, mixed and poured dozens of yards of concrete walls and floors in that basement, tore off the front porch and built a back porch, constructed rock walls, tilled, planted, weeded and harvested a one-acre garden every year, and, most importantly to *us*, built two indoor bathrooms with toilets.

Our weekends were rarely our own and we started early on whatever project struck my father's fancy. We put in a septic system, connected natural gas, re-wired and re-plumbed the entire house. We got rid of the coal furnace and replaced it with a forced air gas furnace and a wood stove.

My father had no training in construction but was curious and fearless and filled the house with how-to books and *Popular Mechanics* magazines. While replacing a set of upstairs windows, he found some termite damage and when my mother returned from grocery shopping, she found an entire side of the two-story house removed, exposing their bedroom to passing cars, like a giant dollhouse dropped into the green countryside.

I can still remember my mother's look of horror as she drove in the driveway to see us waving to her through what had been the solid walls of her bedroom.

BEFORE SUNRISE

"To translate this situation would be like trying to stuff a cloud in a suitcase."
- W. P. Kinsella, *Shoeless Joe*

It was still dark. I was the first one in the transpo van so it was a little awkward. I didn't know the driver; he didn't know me. We were in the parking lot of the Dubuque Best Western and it dawned on me that I could be making a big mistake.

"Is this the van to the *Shoeless Joe* set?"

The movie *Field of Dreams* was originally called *Shoeless Joe*, the title of the book on which it was based.

"Yeah." He shifted in his seat to look at me in the mirror. "Didja think you were in the wrong van?" I could tell he was smiling, even in the dark. His Midwestern accent was thick and familiar and I relaxed.

"It occurred to me."

"That'd be a great way to start the day, eh?" The flat vowels were like butter melting on corn.

Some of the crew guys climbed into the van, looking beat. I noticed from the call sheet that they had just switched from night shoots to days, so everyone was probably still adjusting. I moved to the back with my gym bag, so it was easier for them to get in.

I pulled the script out, even though it was still too dark to read. I had been carrying it around for weeks, as if I could absorb some of the magic of the story by osmosis. I had learned onstage that sometimes it's harder to do a small part, because the tendency is to make each word too precious. I already knew my lines, but the stack of paper felt good in my lap.

I had been given the novel *Shoeless Joe* years earlier by a friend from high school, but I had never dreamed that they would make a movie out of it and that, one day, I would be cast in it.

"Shoeless" Joe Jackson was a real baseball player accused of conspiring to lose the World Series for the Chicago White Sox in1919. The resulting trial was called the Black Sox Scandal, and despite being acquitted of any wrongdoing (Jackson had a Series-leading .375 batting average, with no errors), Shoeless Joe and seven of his teammates were banned from baseball for life.

The novel was a fantasy about Ray Kinsella, an Iowa farmer, obeying a Voice that tells him to build a baseball diamond in the middle of his cornfield, so that Shoeless Joe can magically come back from the dead to play there.

The story was perfect. It reminded me of my dream of becoming an actor, and how crazy that had seemed to everyone I knew in my farming community. Now, here I was, back in the Midwest to shoot a major motion picture—an uplifting story that might inspire other people to follow their dreams.

As the van sped along the interstate, the sun had just cleared the horizon behind us. You could already tell it was going to be a hot one. I remembered this kind of day from baling hay in Ohio, but usually that was in September, not in June. The eight crew members in the van were finally coming to life, and they started to joke with each other about their work at the farm location.

"Maybe we could dig a trench between two of the rows and Kevin could walk in that," said the stocky, unshaven guy two seats ahead of me.

The bearded guy in the passenger seat said something but I couldn't hear it. There were laughs all around.

"That would be great!" said the salt-and-pepper crewcut in front of me. "Or he could walk on his knees." More laughs.

It was hard to hear them from the back seat with the big guy next to me snoring, but it sounded like they were talking about the corn. I looked out the window and the first rays of sun exposed the stunted corn in the endless fields around us. I vaguely remembered hearing about the drought conditions on the television in my hotel room the night before.

I tried to imagine the scenes with the ballplayers walking out of a cornfield with the waist-high rows of corn stalks I was seeing out the window. It just wouldn't work. Maybe Kevin Costner would have to walk through the corn on his knees to make it look taller. I smiled to myself.

I am about to be in a baseball movie with Kevin Costner.

In July of 1989, I was shopping in a cramped, corner grocery store in Bodfish, California, a small town of 2,000 people near the Kern River where I had spent the weekend camping. I was strolling the aisles, unshaven and smelling of wood smoke, when I made eye contact with a stocky, round-faced man in his late thirties, who also happened to be in the produce section, shopping with his cart.

It was the briefest of encounters but we each nodded an acknowledgment in that way that men do to pleasantly but quickly end the awkwardness of looking another man in the eyes. I passed on to the soup aisle.

Two minutes later, as I was perusing the tea section, I noticed the same man was approaching again from the other end of the aisle. He was looking at me with a quizzical expression on his face. I studied the tea.

I could see from the corner of my eye that he was slowing down as he came near me, so I casually dropped my pretense of looking for a hot beverage and met his eyes. He still had the questioning look on his face, but he stared at me without speaking. "Hey," I said, all friendly-like.

He paused a bit longer. "Do I know you?" he offered slowly.

Having never had a great memory for faces, I was immediately on the defensive. *Do I know this guy and just can't remember him?* I hate when this happens. I smiled and prepared a look of recognition in case it came to me, and then set about scouring my mind for clues as to who this stocky, freckled man might be. *Nothing.* We stared at each other shaking our heads like reflections in a fun house mirror.

"Did we go to high school together?" he tried next.

"I don't think so. I went to high school in Ohio," I replied.

His face went dark and then brightened in an instant. "You look like that guy from *Field of Dreams*," he blurted. Relief spilled on to his face, the mystery solved. "Anybody ever tell you that?" he added apologetically.

"Yeah," I said, finally relieved of my task of trying to place this man's face in my memories. The little man seemed smaller now as he shuffled backwards, bumping into his shopping cart.

"Sorry, man," he mumbled.

"It's okay." I smiled, trying to cover my glint of pride at being recognized in public. "I *am* that guy."

"No way."

"Yeah, " I assured him.

"No way. Really?"

"Yep. That was me," I said.

"Really?" He stared at me skeptically, resting his hand on his shopping cart.

It felt strange now, trying to convince this guy that I was exactly who he thought I was. My stomach growled and I remembered why I had left my campsite in the first place. I was about to offer a handshake and get back to finding my breakfast when his face darkened   and tears sprouted in the corners of his eyes.

"I can't believe this," he whispered and he lurched backwards slightly, as if he had suddenly lost his balance. His eyes grabbed deeply at mine. "Unbelievable…"

"What?" I asked quietly. The other shoppers in the aisle were politely moving away from us.

"I can't believe it's you," he sputtered. I stood in the aisle for a long moment, my arms tingling, wondering whether I should hug this little bear of a man or run away from him.

"Can I tell you something?" he whispered. It felt like he was asking himself whether he really wanted to tell me, rather than whether I wanted to hear it.

"Sure," I said.

"When that movie came out, I went to see it because I love baseball. I used to play…" He sucked in his stomach and trailed off, looking at his feet.

"But all's I could think about while watching it was my dad," and again he stopped. This time, he wanted to continue but it was clear his voice would not let him. His mouth started his next words twice without sound, before he looked up to the ceiling and cleared his throat. "My dad…" he finally said, "My dad and me didn't really get along too well."

I looked down into his pleading eyes and nodded involuntarily. The grocery basket pulled heavily on my arm. It felt like he was forcing himself to look at me now, for fear that if he turned away I might disappear and he would be left alone in the grocery aisle with his tears.

"I want to tell you this," he continued, calmer now. "I hadn't spoken to my dad in 15 years, and after I saw that movie, I drove up to Bakersfield and I just grabbed him by the arm and asked him to come with me. He was so surprised, he just got in the car. We sat and watched that movie together and that was it. We just stopped being mad at each other. Just realized, I guess, how stupid it was." He stared off for a moment, as if looking in his memory for any traces of his old resentment.

"That movie changed my life," he sighed, "I just wanted to tell you that."

His eyes danced quickly from the linoleum floor to the water-stained ceiling, avoiding me on the way. His strong, freckled hand grabbed his face, smeared both eyes with one swipe and wiped it roughly on his jeans. His eyes darted to mine with something of a challenge and his chin dimpled and quivered in spasms.

"Thank you," I said, meeting his eyes and offering my hand. "I'm Dwier. What's your name?"

His eyes surrendered. "I'm Tommy. Thomas." He grabbed my hand and pulled me toward him and we ended up in one of those awkward "man" hugs where our hands were still clasped between us while our free hands gently thumped the other man's back.

By now, the three older fishermen buying bait were actively ignoring the crying men embracing in the grocery store while at the same time trying to squeeze around us to continue their shopping.

"You want me to show you how to play baseball?"

"Baseball is ninety percent mental and the other half is physical."
-Yogi Berra

It was summer and my brother and sister and I were in the field by our house with the new bat and ball we had gotten for Christmas.

This was a real horsehide baseball with perfect red stitching pulled impossibly tight around the core, as if it was holding in some unstable power source. The bat was our first full-sized Louisville Slugger. It was pale yellow and probably more bat than we could handle, but, as was the custom of the age, Santa Claus brought us things that he knew we would grow into. We had spent the long months since Christmas carefully wrapping, then re-wrapping the grip of the bat with Dad's electrical tape until we got it just right.

Dad was at work and my eight-year old sister Barb was trying to get my older brother (Ferris was six) and me (five) to play a little game of pitch and hit.

Barb was a bit of a tomboy back then, and, as the oldest, took great pleasure in bossing us around. The preferred method my brother Ferris and I had devised to assert ourselves was to stick together and present a unified front of resistance to whatever plan she was hatching for us.

It must have been working that day, because my mother, who had been inside washing the breakfast dishes, heard us complaining and came out to see what was the matter.

As soon as we saw her emerge from the house, we figured we were in trouble. Ferris and I launched into our joint complaint that Barb was trying to tell us what to do while my exasperated sister explained.

"I was only trying to get them to stand in the right places so we could play!"

"No you weren't!" I argued.

"She wasn't gonna let us bat!" Ferris added.

"That's not true," Barb intoned righteously, "I was just trying to show them how to do it right."

"We know how to bat," my brother offered.

"Yeah!" I said, hoping to have the final word.

Mom looked at us with that "Are you finished?" look on her face and we quickly fell silent. After a long moment, Mom slowly pried the brand new bat from my brother's white-knuckled hand and walked a few more steps into the open field.

We watched with mouths agape, wondering what she would do next. Would she toss the bat as far as she could into the weeds? Would she forbid us to use it until we learned how to get along?

My mother was not an athlete. She was an only child, raised in a small Ohio town on the West Virginia border. Because she was home alone so often with her mother, they were very close, and my mother spent most of her time reading and playing with her dolls. My grandfather was a stern man who worked constantly and spent his few leisure hours listening to baseball games on the radio. My mother believed that if she had only had someone, anyone, to play with as a child, she would never have argued with them.

After a few steps, she turned around and we waited for her verdict.

She eyed us calmly. "You want me to show you how to play baseball?"

"*You're* gonna play with us?" I asked, incredulous.

"Why not?," she asked calmly.

"Yippee!" we all squealed. This was a special day for sure. In our excitement, we danced around like moths on a light bulb.

Mom instructed us where to go. "Barb, you pitch the ball to me. Ferris, you go out in the field and Ricky (she called me by my childhood nickname), you stand behind me and be the catcher." It didn't occur to me at the time that Mom was protecting me by putting me behind her, out of the way of any hard grounders or line drives.

The catcher! I thought, *What a great idea, Mom.* Who knew our mom was so smart about baseball? We had never thought to have a catcher before. With only three of us, we had always only had enough players for a pitcher, a batter and a fielder. The batter always had to drop the bat and run to retrieve any pitches that he hadn't been able to hit, which was a lot of them. Now, as the official catcher, I was there to catch them. This would speed up our game considerably.

You could tell my mother was excited, too. She was always happy to play with us inside, but, when it came to outside games, she usually sat on a blanket and watched. Now she was right out here with us and we all felt good about it.

Mom stood next to the worn-down spot in the grass we had designated as home plate. I crouched proudly behind her. She looked sturdy in her exaggerated batting stance, her long, pale legs stretched across our imaginary batter's box. Behind her, in the distance, I saw my sister looking determined, standing at attention on the weathered two-by-four we called the pitcher's mound, our one and only baseball in her hand. Even farther behind her, impossibly far away on the expanse of green, my brother danced into his position. None of us knew how hard Mom could hit, but she looked good in her stance and I was happy that Ferris was taking no chances by playing her deep.

The moment is etched in my brain, a Polaroid image that is always developing in my mind's eye, the telescoping figures of my mother's bat-laden back emerging from the void in the foreground, my squinting sister in the middle ground and my big brother poised in the distance on a sea of green.

My sister starts into a comically elaborate wind-up and from the distance I hear my brother start his chatter—"Hey, batter, batter, Hey, bat-ter..."—as he hunkers into his stance, his head turned slightly to the right to favor his good eye.

As the pitch approaches, my mother's leg muscles tighten and the bat lifts off from her shoulder. She, too, is caught up in the excitement of the moment and swings hard. She narrowly misses the ball and as her bat completes its swing, a flash of white light explodes in my head and I find myself looking up at the sky. My mother's voice whispers "Oh my gosh" and her silhouetted face appears above me. I feel her cool hands on my cheeks and I can taste blood in my mouth. Mom looks me hard in my eyes and asks, "Are you alright?"

My sister's face appears and asks matter-of-factly, "Why did you hit Ricky with the bat?" Mom ignores this, and by the time Ferris arrives from the outfield asking, "What happened?" I am in my mother's arms and we are walking swiftly toward first base. In my delirium, I imagine we are playing a whole new kind of baseball where bloody children are carried around the base paths, a kind of game with rules that grown-ups have kept secret from us. After we pass first base, we continue walking straight down the imaginary foul line toward our neighbor's house.

Mrs. Ulrich is a chain-smoking science teacher with a gravelly voice and a short beehive hairdo. She and her husband have three children close to our ages but we are new to the neighborhood and barely know them. At her kitchen door, Mom explains breathlessly that my dad has our car at work and that I got hurt playing baseball and need to go to the doctor's. Mrs. Ulrich casually sets down her beanbag ashtray, exhales a long plume of smoke, and comes over to examine my bloody mouth.

"Gees," she says, "that's a lot of blood." She pulls my face away from the blood now drying on my mother's crisp, cotton blouse. "I don't see any cut on the outside, what happened?"

Mom's too impatient to explain, but she is nothing if not polite. "I wanted to show the kids how to play baseball so I went out... I didn't realize Ricky was standing so close behind me and I accidentally hit him in the mouth."

"With the bat?" Mrs. Ulrich tries to hide her surprise. She opens my red-rimmed mouth and pokes around in the bloody saliva. Her fingers taste like metal. It doesn't hurt too much but the blood is disconcerting to me. I want to keep crying but I'm distracted by the dizzy feeling in my head. "Let me get some cotton," Mrs. Ulrich says as she walks to the bathroom, plucking her cigarette from the ashtray as she goes.

Alone with family for a moment, Ferris repeats the question he has been asking *ad nauseum* in the background since our once-hopeful game ended so abruptly: "What happened?"

Mom finally lets her hidden panic show with an uncharacteristic, "Hush!"

Ferris slinks away and quietly whispers to our sister, "What happened?"

"Hush!" Barb says.

Mrs. Ulrich returns with cotton balls and stuffs a few into my left cheek and says, "Let's go."

Mom looks relieved to finally be on our way and we all climb into Mrs. Ulrich's black Corvair. The pain in my mouth is getting sharper, but the big, blood-soaked cotton balls taste like pennies and are comforting to poke at with my tongue. I like looking up at my mom and she strokes my forehead as we ride. I feel proud that my mother looks a bit like Jackie Kennedy when she smiles. She is trying hard to smile now...

I don't remember much about my visit to the doctor's office, but by the time we left I had nine stitches on the inside of my left cheek and my mouth was filled with fresh cotton. I guess my mom's follow-through had knocked my left cheek into my teeth, which had cut the inside of my mouth.

Despite the embarrassment of having to recount the story endlessly to the doctor's staff, Mom was relieved that it hadn't done more damage.

"You want me to show you how to play baseball?" quickly became a family joke that would evoke mock horror anytime she offered to teach us a new skill, like, "You want me to show you how to trim your hair?" "...mow the lawn?" "...use that chain saw?"

When my dad got home from work that night, Mom must have quickly filled him in with the embarrassing details of her "child abuse." After giving me a quick once over and smiling gamely at my swollen cheek, Dad just tussled my hair and said, "I guess I'll have to teach you how to play catch."

CATCH

"The whole reason little boys bring gloves to baseball games and old boys never do:
Because through baseball they have learned what they can reasonably expect from life."
- David Hinckley

The Shoeless Joe van finally turned north off the interstate onto a smaller paved road. There were nothing but farms, now, and they were getting farther and farther apart. Through the van's tinted windows I saw the first glow of dawn creeping across the cornfields. I took the script off my lap and slid it back into my gym bag.

My hand brushed against the old mitt I had brought from my parent's house for luck. I pulled it out of the bag. The worn leather felt soft and cool in my grip. It had only a single leather shoelace strung between the thumb and forefinger for webbing.

The big guy sitting next to me, who had been sleeping almost since the moment he climbed into the van, woke up inexplicably and tried to focus his bleary eyes on the swollen glove that was in my hand.

"Is that from the prop department?"

"No, it's my dad's mitt. From when he was a kid." I held it up for him to see.

"Cool." I didn't feel like letting go of it right then, so I hoped he wouldn't ask to hold it.

"He must be excited for you to be working on a baseball movie. My dad is stoked."

"Mine too," I said before I realized it. This was not the first time I had pretended my dad was still alive, but it surprised me nonetheless. It had only been a month since he'd died—thirty-six days to be exact—and I could not get used to the fact that I would never see him again. I turned his mitt over in my hand.

My father had taught my brother and me to catch with this mitt. It looked like a tan leather version of one of Mickey Mouse's gloves rather than a modern mitt. Catching with it hadn't been easy. Dad taught us to use our free hand to cover the ball once it hit the old mitt, since there was no way to "close" the glove around the ball. I'd throw the ball back to Dad and then toss the mitt to my brother for his turn. We got pretty good at catching with both hands, but it was tedious to have to share the old split-finger glove.

Determined to buy our own mitts, we washed cars and sold Kool-Aid in the front yard of the duplex we lived in on a quiet, suburban street in Uniontown, Ohio, before we moved to the farm.

So it was a big day when we took our saved allowances to buy baseball mitts at Sears. We tried on every glove they had on display and, like the brothers we were, we picked mitts that were similar but not the same. Both were too big for us. My brother chose a Bob Gibson model, while I opted for one endorsed by my hero, Roberto Clemente.

While dancing around the aisles of Sears, shagging ghost flies, we wiggled our tiny fingers deep into the virgin gloves and pounded our fists into the palms roughly, testing the padding and imagining the deep line drives that would go there to die. I dreamed of seeing my picture in the Baseball Hall of Fame, along with the faces of my heroes on baseball cards, many of which I'd carefully cut out of the back of cereal boxes.

We left the mitts on our hands until our fingers were sticky with sweat, while my father looked for his salvation in the tool aisles. On the drive home, I wore my glove over my face like a knight's visor, feeling invincible, looking out the car windows through the holes in the webbing and becoming intoxicated with the smell of new leather.

As we pulled into our driveway, we burst out of our 1960 Ford station wagon before the wheels had stopped rolling and ran around until I found our grass-stained baseball where we had left it in the corner of the lawn. I lobbed it to my brother and he held up his brand new mitt to catch it. The ball landed squarely in the glove, but when he looked to admire his handiwork, the ball rolled out of the stiff leather and onto the ground.

Dad brought out his old mitt to play with us. It was faded with age and you could barely read the autograph of "Johnny Moore" embossed into the leather palm. I had never heard of him. My brother and I stood opposite him and he took turns tossing the ball to us, one at a time, giving us advice as he went. "Keep your mitt up. Thatta boy! Don't be afraid of the ball. Bend your knees a little bit. Aw, almost got it. Don't worry, you'll catch the next one. Keep your eye on the ball. That's it. Protect your face."

My father would catch as many of our wild throws as possible with his old-fashioned glove, two-handed in the style of the old-time players he had grown up with. His body would duck and lean empathetically as he watched us struggle with our oversized, stiff, new mitts.

What I know now that I didn't know then is that my father was not a great baseball player. He had grown up six blocks from the beach in New Jersey and when he wasn't working to help out his family, he had spent all of his spare time swimming in the ocean. When he was five, he had been tossed off the pier by his father and told to "Sink or swim!" Fortunately, Dad opted for a gentler method of coaching.

He knew the basic rules of baseball and football and how to play, but he was not the kind of father who could teach us how to throw a curveball or improve our swing, the way he would teach us the finer points of the backstroke and that the proper way to enter the cold Atlantic for a swim was to run screaming and dive. He played catch with us until we were competent and then let our brotherly competitiveness take over.

He taught us a game he had played as a kid, called "Worky-up," which was handy when you didn't have enough players for a game. One player was the batter and he would toss the ball up and hit it. The other players in the field would get points for catching the hit: one point for grounders, two points for fly balls. The first fielder to ten points would win his turn to bat while the others all started at zero again. The game taught us to be pretty aggressive fielders, and it was an endless one we could play with the neighbor kids—before the farm, when we still had neighbors.

Before we went to bed, Dad brought out the saddle soap from the family shoeshine kit and showed us how to use it to soften the leather. My brother and I took turns sleeping with the baseball in the glove, shoved under our pillow, to help it form into the perfect "basket." To this day, the creamy smell of saddle soap has a mildly sedative effect on me.

Once in bed, my brother and I would lie under the cool sheets on hot summer nights and whisper to each other in the space between the wall and our bunk beds which we called the "peep hole," until one of us would submerge in sleep from the day's exertions, sometimes fading out in mid-whisper.

.000

"If I tried for them dinky singles I could've batted around six hundred."

- Babe Ruth

The movie van bounced, and I could feel stones hit the wheel wells under my feet. Outside, a cloud of dust was following us and I realized we had transitioned to gravel roads. *Wow, this farm must really be "out there."*

I wormed my hand into my father's old mitt. The leather inside was still smooth and soft. Dad would be proud. The finger holes were a little short for my hands now, but feeling my hand in that mitt along with the flutter of excitement and nervousness in my belly reminded me of riding to Little League games as a boy.

Maybe I've finally made it to the Big Leagues.

"Did you see Costner hit it into the corn yesterday?" The voice came from the front of the van. Grunts of assent.

"Yeah, that was a hell of a shot!" said a guy with long, dark hair two rows up.

"It didn't even look like he was trying!"

I felt my stomach tighten. I hadn't met Kevin yet, but I had been hoping that he was no better than I was at baseball. I was glad that I had taken a few trips to the batting cages since finding out I'd gotten the part. The production company had told me that my character, John Kinsella, wouldn't be required to bat, but I knew firsthand how things can change once you're on the set and the cameras are rolling. I wanted to be ready.

I was not too worried about playing catch. My dad had taught me the fundamentals, my brother and I had played catch a million times as kids, and I had learned the finer points in Little League.

When I was nine years old and starting Little League baseball at my new school, I had been assigned to the White Sox team, coached by a wiry, middle-aged mechanic named Mr. Rinehart. Mr. Rinehart was a temperamental, demanding coach who stalked the baselines like a big league manager. He was a no-nonsense, competitive, tobacco-spitting tornado of a man with a West Virginia drawl I could barely understand.

Mr. Rinehart knew baseball and saw in me a good fielder with a decent arm, but one who was prone to daydreaming and distraction. I could become so preoccupied with fantasies of winning the game single-handedly that I would lose sight of the actual game unfolding in front of me.

All through the pre-season practice period, I did fine. Coach Rinehart put us through his drills. We played "pepper" and shagged flies and did fielding practice where Coach would yell out real game scenarios seconds before he would hit the ball into the infield. "One out, runner at second" or "Bases loaded, no outs," he would gargle out around his cheek full of tobacco. "Atta boy, Dwar." "Keep them throws up! C'mon boys, don't make 'im dig it out th' dirt!"

Once the season started, however, I had a problem—I couldn't get a hit. By the third game of the season, no matter how hard I tried, I couldn't get my bat to connect. I don't know if it was watching my older brother steadily move up the batting order, but the more I thought about my hitting drought, the more hopeless I felt.

I could hit okay in practice, but come game time, to use Coach Rinehart's words, it felt like I "was swangin' a toothpick at a BB."

The farther into the season my slump went, the closer the fathers got to me. My dad tried to help me. Coach Rinehart tried to help me. Even some of my teammates' fathers would offer casual advice as they patted me on the back after a game. "Keep your eyes on the ball," or "You're grippin' the bat pretty tight," and, my favorite, "Relax up there, son."

How was I supposed to relax when I was humiliating myself in front of everyone in my new town?

Coach Rinehart would stand behind me after practice and put his oil-stained mechanic's hands over mine on the bat and show me how to time my swing, while his son Ricky pitched to us. Calmly, he would whisper over my shoulder, the sour, sweet smell of his Red Man tobacco forming a cloud around us, "Thar it is…Wait fer it…Wait fer it…Swang!"

Ricky, who was a standout pitcher on the high school team and something of a smartass, would sometimes try to sneak me his curveball or a slider, and Coach Rinehart would stand up and scream, "Ricky! Throw th' dam' ball over the plate!" But he would speak gently to me, in hushed, inspiring tones.

My father, who could offer me little but encouragement, put in extra time throwing me pitches in our backyard as I stood in front of our Pitchback, which would stop the balls that got by me. He would sometimes toss them underhand, occasionally substituting a softball, hoping that it would be easier for me to hit.

My father's advice was always the same: "If at first you don't succeed, try, try again." It occurs to me that fathers are at their best when there is something to overcome, something to fix.

With all the extra work, I became a better hitter in practice, but the games were still another story. In spite of all the attention (or maybe because of it), I continued my slump, finishing that entire Little League season batting .000.

That was almost twenty years ago. And although I played many more seasons of baseball with respectable batting averages, sometimes I am still haunted by the ghost of my Little League Triple-Zero Summer.

I hadn't ridden in a van with my hand in a mitt since I was twelve. For all the times I'd done that as a boy, it seemed funny that I'd never done it again until this trip to the *Shoeless Joe* set. I felt the old leather squeeze my fingers. I wished in that moment that understanding my father could have been as simple as putting on his glove. It would have made our relationship so much easier.

I had brought my father's mitt to Iowa with me so that I could wear it in the movie as a tribute to him. Just a little secret between him and me. He would have loved that. My dad had kept a few secrets. He could be defined more by the things he *didn't* talk about, than by things he did.

I studied the mitt. *I can't believe I learned how to catch with this thing.*

The "Johnny Moore" signature that had been embossed on the leather palm was like a ghost now and Johnny Moore himself had probably been dead for decades. I wonder if his son had trouble grieving, too.

It was not even the letting go that was difficult. Even though I had held my father's hand when he died, I hadn't been able to "feel" his death because it didn't seem like he was really gone. A therapist would probably have called it "denial," but it felt to me like he was still around, flying around like the birds he always loved to watch, painting sunsets on the sky now, just like the ones he had painted on canvases. When I pictured him, he felt free. I just couldn't cry about it.

And that worried me.

Here I was, minutes away from arriving on the set of my "dream" movie—the most exciting job I had ever gotten. I had been hired to play a father coming back from the dead to play catch with his son one last time. But I just couldn't feel emotional about it. For all the times my father had told me, "Don't cry, or I'll give you something to cry about," now, finally, I *had* something to cry about and I just couldn't find the tears.

"My daddy died before I was born," she said.

"He was killed on the first day of the Tet offensive in Vi't Nam in January of 1968. He was 19 years old. Drafted four months out of high school, dead three months later. I was born in May. I'm a Taurus." She changed tracks abruptly. "Can I tell you a story?"

I nodded. I didn't know where this was going, but this spirited little woman wasn't about to let me walk back to my table once she had guessed who I was, even if it meant her stepping out of the bathroom line for a moment. I couldn't place her heavy drawl exactly, but I guessed Texas.

I had admitted I was in *Field of Dreams*. "I knew it!" she had said, loudly, causing an older woman also standing in line to glance at us discretely. "I knew it was you!" Feisty repeated. I smiled tentatively.

"I guess the first few years were pretty hard on my mama, raisin' me by herself and missin' my dad. But we lived with my dad's parents and my dad's best friend from high school was around a lot to help out."

"I got older and started playin' softball and I started askin' about my dad, and Uncle Dave, (that was what I called my dad's friend), he would tell me stories about him--what a great guy he was and so much fun—" each sentence came out of her mouth faster than the last, like a train picking up steam— "and I loved hearin' the stories 'cuz Mama would always get sad when I asked her, so it was kinda perfect." I found myself trying to calm her down by breathing deeply myself.

"But what was funny was, even as a little girl I couldn't really see my dad in the stories, I just really liked hearin' 'em. I had a fantasy about him that he loved baseball and that's why *I* loved baseball, and it was just this little secret I had with my dad. Uncle Dave would take me to practices and come to all my games and my little secret made me play harder and harder 'cuz I knew it was like my dad was playin' through me, y'know what I mean?"

I nodded.

"I played really well my senior year and I got a softball scholarship to college and I played all four years and it was great. My Uncle Dave came to all my games and my mom came to as many as she could, but then I graduated and I got a job in Houston and I got real busy with my life.

"I missed playin' softball and I realized that what I really missed was my secret bond with my dad. So it was weird but, here I was twenty years old and, for the first time in my life, I really missed my dad. Is this okay?—I can't believe I'm tellin' you all this…"

By now I had forgotten that my friend, left alone at our table, might be wondering what was taking so long in the men's room. "It's okay," I said.

"Well, it's a good thing you're standin' up 'cuz I'm talking the legs right off your chair." She laughed apologetically.

"It's okay. What happened?"

"I'll cut to the chase. So, I came home for my twenty-first birthday and I'm tellin' my Uncle Dave that I'm missin' softball and he says 'Why don't we go see this movie? I heard it's about baseball. Maybe it'll make you feel better.' So, I say 'Okay,' and we go, just him and me.

"Well, that movie…" For a moment, she is speechless, shaking her head. "It starts out and I'm just lovin' it. I'm hearin' the voices and buildin' the field right with him. And Costner's on the tractor and his daughter's right there with him talkin' baseball and, and it's like my whole father fantasy thing is happenin' right in front of me.

"And I start to get a little scared and a little teary-eyed, like maybe it's gonna end or somethin's gonna ruin it and I grab my Uncle Dave's hand in the dark, just to have something to hold onto. And he's just watchin' the movie real quiet-like. And Shoeless Joe appears and Kevin goes off to find Moonlight Graham and I'm totally with them.

"Then the little girl chokes on the hotdog and I'm like—I'm the little girl, that's me!" Feisty says this extra loud, for emphasis, and a waiter in the kitchen looks up from his order pad. "And then Kevin holds her, and Doc Graham saves her and I'm thinkin' the movie's over.

"Next thing I know, there *you* are and my mouth just drops open and I start cryin' again and I feel Uncle Dave's hand kinda shakin' and I'm like, I never *seen* Uncle Dave cry before. He's squeezin' my hand kinda hard and I pull my hand away from him and put it on his shoulder to comfort him and that just makes him cry harder. So I don't know what to do.

"The movie ends and he's still cryin' and we're both a little shaken up. We sit there for a while until we can manage to pull ourselves together and we walk outside. And he's kinda quiet so I start talkin'—I tend to talk a lot when I get emotional--" (I nod slowly, like I'm surprised) "—and I say something like 'Wow, that movie really reminded me of my dad...'" and Uncle Dave stops suddenly, like he walked into a plate glass window, and he turns to me and he looks me right in the eye, takes a deep breath and he says, *'I'm* your dad.'

"And I'm lookin' at him and I'm thinkin' *Does he mean he's* like *a dad to me or...?*

"My mind is racing, but I'm lookin' at him and I can tell by the look in his eye and the way his lips are quivering that it's true. He says 'I'm sorry...' real quiet and he's got this pleading look in his eyes. I just walked away and got in the car and he got in the car and we started drivin' home, neither one of us sayin' anything.

"I think he was afraid I would be mad, and I guess I was, but in that moment I was just in shock. I had just seen my "father fantasy" finally come true before my eyes in this movie and then found out that it wasn't really my father after all. I wanted to be mad, but I couldn't figure out what to be mad *at*. I guess it kinda made sense why I had never been able to put the photos of my 'dad' into my fantasy of him.

"Finally, Dave broke the silence and said, 'I always wanted to tell you but I didn't know how. Your mom and I, we…uh…had a thing… one night about three weeks after Tim shipped out from Ft. Polk. We were drunk and scared about him goin' to war and we both missed him and we felt horrible about it afterward.

"'Well, two months later, your mom figures out she's pregnant and writes Tim this excited letter to tell him. A week later, she gets notified that he was killed. We were all devastated. Tim's parents were heartbroken, and when your mom told them she was pregnant, they insisted she move in with them. Everyone was so excited to have you— me included—to have a part of Tim to hold onto, that your mom and I just never talked about it. It was hard enough to cope without dredgin' up that mess.'

"Dave said that the older I got, the more sure he became that I was his daughter but he didn't know how to tell everyone. He figured my grandparents would be devastated—not just that I wasn't really their granddaughter but that he had slept with my mom while her husband, their son, was gettin' ready to go to war. He didn't even know how Mama would react after all these years, so he just kept bein' my "uncle" and hangin' around and pretendin' he didn't know.

"But then we went to see this fantasy baseball movie because I was missing my dad and, lo and behold, I ended up losing my fantasy but finding my dad."

"Wow," I said. I looked blankly at the water fountain, absorbing her story. "That's…" When I looked back to her face, I noticed she was quiet for the first time in the four minutes since I met her. Her face was subtly pleading with me, like she wanted me to tell her what to do. I felt a little responsible somehow. "How did everyone deal with the news?"

She looked at the floor. "We decided not to tell anyone for the time being. I mean, we don't even *know* for sure. But, I've lived so long without a dad, it's kinda nice to think maybe he's been there all along."

"That sounds like a pretty enlightened way to look at it. I'll bet your dad is proud of you." I opened my arms to her and she hugged me tightly. She made a squeaking noise like a puppy into my chest.

She hugged me for a long time, with the new women in the bathroom line looking at us out of the corners of their eyes. Her strong, little arms felt good around my waist. When she finally pulled away, she looked at my shirt. "Oh my gosh," she giggled, "I cried all over you…"

Back on the Farm

"Life is best in a state of hopeful anticipation."

- Tammy Noble

The van finally slowed down on the washboard road and took a right turn into a long, gravel driveway. As we turned, I got a glimpse of the white farmhouse huddled under a large barn of faded red. I bobbed around in my seat in an effort to see around the heads of my van mates, who were not nearly as excited as I was. The stones hitting the undercarriage of the van mirrored the tap dance my feet were doing.

Riding down that long driveway the first time was a thrill. I was watching the story I had read in the script and imagined from the novel come to life before my eyes like a long tracking shot in a movie. When the van crossed the tiny bridge and moved into the parking lot, I saw the ballfield for the first time, perfect in its simplicity and striking in its placement. In the early light, the grass seemed almost unnaturally green.

The smell of creek and soil and grass hit my nose before my feet hit the gravel lot. I stood and inhaled. Everything about it was a rush of nostalgia. The sweet smell of the creek just behind us, the freshly-cut grass, the dust still settling around me: all of it whispered to me of how I missed this farm, this farm I was only seeing now for the first time.

All of my fellow passengers went off to their work, and I was alone in the parking lot. I looked up at the farmhouse on the slope above me. It reminded me of my best's friend's farm from childhood, and the flutter of excitement in my chest whenever I walked there after my work at home was finally done. I passed the grip trucks and dressing room trailers at base camp and stepped onto the porch by the back door.

For me, it was like a dream come true: the culmination of childhood puppet shows in our basement, the sweaty, one-act plays and bawdy melodramas in the stuffy Sharon Center town hall as a teenager, my vaguely obscene "honey bun" dance in my high school production of *South Pacific* and even the crazy nights of improv in front of drunken Midwestern college crowds. Here I was, eight years later, back on a farm, to help tell a magical story about following your dreams.

From the quiet moan of the screen door, I knew I was home. It was a classic two-story farmhouse with creaky wood floors tilted slightly from the settling of the foundation's stones into the rich, loam soil.

As if I needed more evidence that I had returned to my childhood home, the farmhouse was, at present, a massive construction zone. The film crew was completely renovating the house for the movie, doing much of the same work I had done with my father on our farm as a young man— tearing down walls, building a porch, putting in windows.

The lingering smell of sawdust and plaster particles and the sight of the exposed, oak wall studs, darkened with age, took my body back twenty years in an instant.

I could see the marks on the floors where the production crew had removed walls to make it easier to maneuver the cameras inside and give the house a more open feeling. I walked through these former "walls" like a ghost, remembering my own youth spent knocking down the lath and plaster walls of our farmhouse and shoveling the enormous piles of rubble out the window.

I found myself staring at the staircase that led up the middle of this strangely familiar farmhouse. How many mornings had I walked down

steep, wooden stairs like the ones in front of me? How many evenings had
I come home, sweaty and sticky with dirt and chaff from helping a neighbor bale his hay fields, to plod up similar stairs and shower off the day?

Out of the corner of my eye, I thought I saw my father standing
by the basement door, in his holey work t-shirt with sawdust in his hair,
puzzling over the next remodeling task. When I turned to look, there was
no one there.

"You can go on up if you want to." I hadn't even heard the guy come
into the room. He was standing by the back door looking at me. He had
a knowing grin on his face and a short barber shop haircut.

"No, I was just looking for the production office."

"Ain't that what they call that trailer in the driveway?" His rural
accent sounded more like Minnesota than Iowa.

"Oh, I must have walked right by it." I started to move toward the
door.

"I'm Don Lansing," the man said. "I own this farm." He held out
his hand with a look of anticipation. I grabbed it and felt the familiar firm
grip and hard calluses of a lifetime of hard work.

"Wow. Congratulations. This is a beautiful farm," I said. His face
erupted into a toothy smile. I guessed he was in his mid-forties but when
he smiled, he turned fifteen. "I'm Dwier. I'm one of the actors." He was
still pumping my hand.

"Are you famous?"

"No, I'm afraid not."

"That's okay. It's good to meet ya, anyways. I was born in this
house, y'know. I can show you around if you want. I mean, if it's okay with
them carpenter guys." He laughed to himself that he had to have permission to be in his own house.

"I just got here, so I should probably check in with the production
office first."

"Well, anything you need, you let me know. I'm livin' in a trailer out by the barn."

"Thank you." He shook my hand again and I walked out smiling to myself. His innate sweetness reminded me of the farmers I used to bale hay for when I was a teenager. Except for that smile. Whenever I went to a neighbor's farm to work, there was never much time for smiling.

No Way Out But Up

"You don't have to deserve your mother's love.
You have to deserve your father's."
- Robert Frost

The morning sun hit me full in the face as I headed out the back door of the Lansing house to find the production trailer from which the line producer supervises the filming. Blinded by the bright sun, I nearly ran into a cluster of people walking toward the door I had just exited.

"Oh, sorry," I said as I backed up, shielding my eyes from the light. I recognized the director from my audition two months ago, despite the sun behind him creating a halo out of his curly hair and cap. "Mr. Robinson."

"Please, it's Phil. I already feel old enough." He smiled as he looked at me for a second. "You're the father, right?"

"Yes, I'm Dwier."

"Dwier Brown, right?" I nodded. "Well, welcome to Iowa."

Phil had large blue eyes and although his voice was soft and melodic, he had an alertness that, like his accent, was all New York. He spoke precisely, like a doctor or a scientist, but his presence in conversation wrapped you up like a favorite blanket. "What do you think so far?"

"I love it. I grew up on a farm in Ohio, so it feels like home to me."

"Well, lucky you." His grin betrayed that he was missing city life. "We're a little behind schedule, but we'll get to you soon." He was already moving toward the house with the small group following him like baby ducks. "We have to decide what to do with his hair..." his voice trailed off as the screen door slammed behind them and I moved again toward the trailers in base camp.

After checking in at the production trailer, I was shown to my dressing room. This was a section of a truck trailer that is divided into eight equal "dressing rooms," each with a built-in couch, a fold-out tabletop and a very small bathroom.

The walls between each room were a bi-fold partition so that your room could be doubled in size if the cast was small or if your career was at a point of success that your agent could negotiate for a larger dressing room. Established "name" actors could sometimes get a double or triple room, the big stars had their own custom motor homes, but because I was the last actor to arrive in Iowa, I ended up with the single room next to the honey wagon.

"Honey wagon" is the affectionate name for the trailer that houses the portable toilets on the set. My star accommodations directly adjacent to that trailer provided yet another olfactory reminder of my childhood.

When my father suddenly moved our family to the old house in the middle of nowhere, the most daunting and annoying feature of our new home was its lack of an indoor toilet. As children, we had all used outhouses before, when camping, but to use one on a daily basis for a year, through rain and snow and dark of night, was a whole new lesson in humility.

As outhouses go, ours looked nothing if not sturdy. It was made of iron—thick, corrugated iron, painted bright red but thoroughly rusted, a two-holer, with one right next to the other, although it was hard to imagine any of us using it simultaneously.

Due to its age and the settling of the ground, the outhouse had a gentle tilt to stern, requiring a little extra effort to stand when your work was done and giving the tiny floor space the angled feel of a tugboat in high seas. Despite the structure's heavy appearance, the tilt gave the user the impression that it could topple over at any moment, and that perhaps the only thing holding the rusted walls together were the spider webs lacing every corner.

The door was huge and heavy, thick iron in an iron frame. Also red and rusted, it hung heavily on its massive hinges and shrieked when it opened, alerting everyone within a half-mile radius. The immense weight of the door, its friction on the jamb, and the vessel's tilt, all conspired to make entering the small chamber a labor of personal strength. Fortunately, no one walked the short path to that door without the adrenalin of immediate need.

The door's "handle" was the hinged metal hasp for a lock that I hope was left over from the door's previous incarnation and not added as a security measure. The overall impression of our iron outhouse was of a strong box, our own private bank vault in the backyard, painted crimson for conspicuousness, and holding treasure of a completely different kind.

The truck drivers who maintained the vehicles parked in base camp did their best to keep the odor of the *Shoeless Joe* honey wagon contained, but with a hundred-man crew working fourteen-hour days in ninety-degree heat—well, you do the math. Needless to say, I wasn't planning to spend a whole lot of time in my dressing room, especially on a beautiful farm like Don Lansing's.

When I returned to the kitchen of the farmhouse on the set, everyone was bustling with activity. Phil and his entourage had already moved on to solve other problems, and I had been asked to wait while Jane, Phil's sweet but serious production assistant walked to the living room to talk to a photographer, who was busy setting up the lights to shoot the image of

Kevin Costner for the movie poster.

To my surprise, she returned with a familiar man sporting a handsome smile. I recognized him as Greg Gorman, one of the best celebrity photographers in the world. "Hi, I'm Greg," he said.

I stood smiling at him, shaking his hand, expecting him to remember me. He didn't. Just as the silence was becoming awkward, Greg looked harder at my face, tilted his head and blurted, "Dwier? Oh my god!" He paused and looked at me again. "What are you doing here?"

"I'm in the movie. I play Kevin's father." His brow wrinkled.

"Are you kidding me? What a coincidence!" He laughed. "Come on in. I'm setting up for Kevin. Let me shoot a headshot for you."

I already knew Greg from having worked with him on a photo shoot. Unfortunately, I wasn't the subject of the photo that time—I was hired as a carpenter to help build some elaborate art deco sets for a photo spread of Bette Midler that Greg had been hired to do for *Life* magazine.

Just two years earlier, frustrated by my inability to get meaningful acting work in Hollywood, I had decided to quit acting and start using the skill I had absorbed from helping my father remodel our farmhouse, the kind of skill that was straightforward and simple and had no pretensions of changing the world—carpentry. I got a job working for an art director.

While I wrestled with giant set pieces rented from the studios and exorcised my frustration by pounding nails to hold them in place, I watched the actors and models, the "talent" as they're called on the set, get treated like visiting royalty.

It was a valuable lesson in humility. I saw from the other side of the camera just how hard everyone else works to make a movie or photo shoot successful. Only after the production crew has been working for hours, days or even months to prepare a shot are the actors brought in to run through their part. Then they are ushered back to their air-conditioned dressing rooms while the crew gets back to work, diligently adjusting any elements that were not camera-ready.

The early mornings and long hours of carpentry work couldn't help but make me think of my father. "Rise and shine!" Dad would yell to us on Saturday mornings to start us moving toward the basement for a day of digging. Each day, my resentment for the work grew.

My father had something of an obsession with digging basements. Having already expanded my grandaddy's root cellar into a full-fledged basement years before, he started us digging a basement under our beat-up farmhouse.

He began by putting support jacks under the floor joists. In our old house the joists were giant logs, mostly unhewn, some still covered in bark, that were secured to the sill at the ends with ten-inch wooden pegs the thickness of a shovel handle. They stretched forty feet from one side of the dirt crawlspace to the other.

We would dig three to four feet down in a large area, remove the dirt with a big wagon, and pour a concrete floor and walls, using a small electric cement mixer. Any rocks we dug up would be washed and thrown into the concrete foundation walls as we built them up from the ground, a few feet at a time. Dad would say, "If you don't like the work, make it into a game." We spent many hours in the damp basement pretending to be Hogan's Heroes, tunneling out of a prison camp.

One day, we uncovered a boulder that was too large to put in a wall and too solid to be broken up into smaller pieces. It was dirty and round like a giant potato, almost four feet long and two and a half feet in diameter. Dad guessed that it weighed 300 pounds and it refused to be broken up with either the sledgehammer or a cold chisel. But he was determined to get it out of his basement.

He wrestled and wrestled with it and, finally, with the help of us kids, Grandaddy and a six foot-long iron crowbar, we managed to roll it to the bottom of the dirt ramp we used to remove the wagonloads of dirt from the basement. The problem with removing anything from a basement is, there is no way out but up.

We heaved and rolled and pried and pushed and moved it a few feet up the ramp and ended up exhausted. *If at first you don't succeed; try, try again.*

The next day, my father started afresh and spent hours moving it another few feet. Like Sisyphus, he would wrestle the boulder up a few inches and it would slide back a few inches. My dad taught us a technique of prying it up with the crowbar and quickly throwing a small rock under it to brace it and then repositioning the crowbar for another heave. It was slow going.

At one point, the boulder turned unexpectedly toward the concrete wall of the cellar ramp and my father, afraid that it might roll all the way back down into the basement, grabbed the boulder as it slammed against the concrete, pinning his hand against the wall. He was in pain, but in typical fashion he was more concerned with keeping the wayward boulder from rolling back into the basement.

He screamed an obscenity or two and we quickly repositioned the crowbar and pried the rock off of his fingers. There was thick, red blood congealing on the back of his dirty hand and two of his fingernails were outlined in blood. He walked into the back yard to wash his hand and cool his temper. The boulder remained on the ramp, halfway out of the basement until the next weekend.

When the rock finally made it up the rest of the ramp, my father insisted on rolling it toward the road, where he had wanted to place something to help visitors to find our driveway. Finally, when Dad had pried the boulder into just the right position next to the ditch, we went back to digging in the basement.

After a few rainstorms and a particularly snowy winter, the dirt washed off our giant basement potato to reveal a beautiful chunk of dark pink granite; moraine left from glaciers that had scraped slowly across northeastern Ohio 30,000 years ago.

The boulder was streaked with thin black bands and flecked with pieces of shiny mica that glistened in the sun. The exterior was rough but the pink color was striking. It remained at the end of the driveway for the next eighteen years.

After months of working hard as a set carpenter and watching the pampered treatment afforded the "talent," I began to imagine my father's voice in my head: "If at first you don't succeed... If you weren't a good carpenter, you wouldn't get any carpentry work. If you want more work as an actor, you will have to work harder at acting." My father's solutions always seemed to involve more work.

Part of the problem was that I had never looked at acting as "work." It had always been fun for me. Acting had been what I had done to avoid work on the farm and I had always felt like performing was my way of getting away with something. I realized that I would have to start taking myself more seriously as an actor before anyone else would.

Even though I had already taken acting classes for years, I signed up for an intense two-year acting program taught by one of Hollywood's best acting teachers, Joanne Baron. It was a hard program to get into, and expensive, and one of the requirements of the studio was that you stop auditioning while you are in class. *How was I supposed to pay for two years of acting class designed to help me get acting work, if I wasn't allowed to take any acting work?* That was where my carpentry skills came in handy...

By the time I auditioned for *Shoeless Joe*, I had completed the first year of the program. It had been a disciplined training, but I had learned how to create a performance consistently and I was gaining confidence as an actor. The program takes summers off, so I was allowed to do the movie, as long as I returned to class in the fall.

Now, here I was, in a farmhouse in Iowa, about to have my headshot taken by one of the most famous celebrity photographers in the world, for a film I was in, after having pounded some nails for that photographer just a year earlier. At that moment, I felt my re-investment in myself as an actor was working out pretty well.

HAIRCUT

"Nobody can be exactly like me. Sometimes even I have trouble doing it."
- Tallulah Bankhead

After using me to stand-in for Kevin while he adjusted the lights and shot my headshot, Jane, the bright P.A. who had brought me to meet Greg, walked quietly into the room. "Time for your haircut!" She had a shy smile.

"I wonder what they're going to do with it," I replied, a little warily. It was summer and I had let it grow out, knowing that they would want to cut it for the movie.

"Don't worry, it'll look great," Greg reassured me as he went back to work, tweaking lights. "I'll give you a print of your headshot tomorrow."

As Jane walked me to the hair and make-up trailer, she informed me that there had been a lot of discussion about what to do with my hair for the film. *What does a character who was born in the 90's and was in his fifties in the 40's but who has been dead for five years in the 70's, look like for a movie that's being shot in the 80's?*

The main problem, I was told by the movie's hair designer, Richard Arrington, was that the next day I was to have a series of still photos taken of me that would accompany Ray Kinsella's voiceover monologue at the opening of the film, and although the photos would span five decades, I would have one haircut.

In the end, it was decided to cut it in a 20's style: shortish on the sides and longish on top to link me with the Shoeless Joe era players.

Sitting in the chair in the makeup trailer with my eyes closed and a haircut apron around me, I felt like a child again. The scary yet comforting buzz of the clippers sent a shiver down my spine.

Until I was in my early teens, my father cut my hair. He would place the tall, metal stool with the pull-out step in the middle of the dining room, grab the Sunbeam hair clippers from the hall closet and wrap a towel around my neck. I could still remember the feel of the cold, metal stool against my shirtless back.

The last haircut my father ever gave me was in 1972. My father was a stickler about fairness with us boys. If my brother got a bike for Christmas, I got a bike for Christmas, and we always got the same haircut. The crewcuts Dad gave us got millimeters longer each year as hairstyles became longer. But that last year of the home haircut, my brother decided to buzz his hair in order to try out for the freshman wrestling team.

When his hair finally grew out, it had changed into large curls. Our respective heads were still covered with the same color and texture of hair, except mine was still straight and his was curly. The buzz haircut was blamed for this phenomenon.

Brothers are naturally competitive with each other, and because my brother, Ferris, is only 14 months older than I am, we were especially so. We have roughly the same build, but he was always taller and stronger and more physically reckless than I was, and he remains so to this day. As a result, most brotherly sporting competitions between us had a predictable result: me, on my back, in pain, begging for mercy.

Frequently, I would get so frustrated and angry at having been beaten that I would throw myself at him in a screaming burst of adrenalized abandon, and immediately find myself on my back again, gasping for breath, under his immovable bulk.

There is only one area where my older brother's physical superiority is compromised. Ferris was born with an eye disorder called amblyopia, or lazy eye, in which his left eye turns inward and requires a strong corrective lens. He has worn glasses since he was one and a half, and had to wear eye patches throughout our childhood to try to improve his vision.

I can't imagine the frustration this condition has caused him, but in typical fashion, Ferris has risen above it and used it to motivate himself to succeed. My brother has always been very competitive and my father was always conscious to offer extra encouragement to Ferris whenever he could.

This made it difficult for me to win my father's approval on the rare occasions I "beat" Ferris at anything. If I won, it was understood that I had had an unfair advantage over him because of his poor vision. If Ferris won, he got additional credit for overcoming his disability and beating me. Winning became a "no win" situation for me.

As a boy, I didn't understand this "exception" to my father's sense of fairness. I unconsciously tried to counter this dynamic by forcing my competitive spirit underground and pretending I wasn't trying to win at all. That way, if I lost, I could save face by claiming that I hadn't even been trying, and if I won, it would be all the more impressive because I had looked so nonchalant in doing so.

Away from the wrestling mats, Ferris began his own game of sneaking up on me around the house and perfecting the latest moves he'd learned at wrestling practice. One day, as I was walking past the downstairs closet to take out the trash, a pile of laundry jumped out of the corner of the closet and twisted my arm behind my back. I pinballed from one side of the hallway to the other, trying to extricate myself from my brother's grasp. In another few seconds, I was on the cold linoleum floor with his leg around my neck, gasping for air. "Give up?" breathed the voice in my ear.

He became like Kato, Closeau's chauffeur in *The Pink Panther*, who attacked his boss at the most random and inappropriate times, so he would learn to always be on guard. And, like Clouseau, I became nervous and paranoid in my own house. But, because of the unspoken code between brothers that you "must" compete at all times, the only solution was to avoid him, which was not easy when we slept in the same room.

"Dad, did you ever fight with your brothers?" I asked my father one day.

I couldn't imagine my father fighting with my Uncle Bill, who was a quiet, bespectacled accountant. We saw my Uncle Bill and his three kids every New Year, but my Uncle Buster was rarely around. Even when we went to visit my father's childhood home in Belmar, New Jersey, near Uncle Buster's house in Monmouth, he was always too busy to spend much time with us.

"Bill and I were pretty close. We had to stick together."

"How about Uncle Buster?" Dad got a faraway look in his eyes. No answer. "And how did he get so rich?" Another long pause.

"That's a long story. All I know is, you'll always have your family."

You got a minute?" It was the Denver airport and I had more than a minute. I had a hundred and twelve of them before my flight left for L.A.

"Uh, sure."

"Aren't you that guy?"

"What do you mean?"

"I recognize you from that movie. *Field of Dreams.*"

"Oh."

"That was a great movie. You got a minute?" I nod. He was an odd mix: pressed slacks but a Clash sweatshirt. I guessed he was a college kid.

"My father was a preacher. I grew up in the church. Went to church every day. Not every day, but services four days a week and then what with Bible studies and prayer circles, I was in that church every day for the first fifteen years of my life. You go to church?"

"Uh, I used to. I was raised Methodist. We went every Sunday, but nothing like what you're talking about."

"Well, I was into it. I knew all the books of the Bible, memorized hundreds of verses. My dad used to love to call me up in front of the congregation or at meetings and throw out verse numbers. He'd say,' Isaiah 16:5', and I'd say, 'The Lord is my Shepherd, blah, blah, blah.' 'Luke 23:12', and I'd say, 'Heed not those whom...' Whatever verse he called out.

"I was like a dog that knew this great trick. He loved it. And I loved doing it because I knew how happy it made him. You ever do that? Just do something to make someone else happy?"

"Yeah, I think we all do that, right?"

"Well, when I was sixteen I stopped doing it. I just realized I didn't want to be that person anymore and I stopped. Dad asked me for a verse during the service one Sunday, and I just pretended I didn't know it. It got real quiet in the sanctuary for a couple of seconds and then he just moved on."

"Wait. Did he know that you knew the verse or did he think he stumped you?"

"Oh, he knew. I could feel it. He knew." His face went blank for a minute as he thought about it. "I don't know why I'm telling you all this."

"It's okay. What happened?"

"We never talked about it. Just sort of pretended it never happened. I went away to college, stopped going to church, went through my whole rebellious phase and, one night, I think it was my junior year—what year did that movie come out?"

"'89."

"Yeah, it was my junior year, and I was drinking with some of my buddies, and we decide to go see this Costner movie. We sneak a couple beers into the movie and we're laughing and joking around at the beginning, but pretty soon we get quiet and we're all into it, right?"

I nod.

"Then the father—" he gestures toward me—"you, show up on the screen and I just about lost it. I didn't breathe for the last five minutes of the movie. I just sat there with tears filling my eyes and I couldn't do anything about it."

"After the movie, my buddies, all these tough guys, I know they all went home and called their dads. I didn't know what to do. It was too late to call my dad and I didn't know what he'd say. I mean, I'd done just what Costner did in the movie: I'd refused to 'play catch' with my dad. Reciting those Bible verses, that was *our* game of catch, and I just stopped doing it. Anyway, I went to bed feeling pretty bad about myself.

"The next day, Sunday morning, I woke up really early and I decided to drive home. I knew I'd arrive during church and I figured I could sneak in the back door and just wait until after the service to talk to him. I had no idea what I was going to say. So I sneaked in the back door and I was waiting in the vestibule and I heard my dad's voice doing the sermon just on the other side of the big, closed swinging doors.

"It felt good to hear his voice again so I leaned closer to hear what he was preaching about. He was talking about a movie he had gone to see last night that he couldn't stop thinking about. I was like, *wow, Dad doesn't go to many movies, I wonder what it was.* And he said, 'It was supposed to be about baseball but it wasn't about baseball. It was about redemption. It's called *Field of Dreams.*' I couldn't believe it!"

"Oh my God," I said, feeling immediately self-conscious.

"He started to go on about the movie and I decided to slip through the swinging doors and sit in the back. Well, as soon as I stuck my head through the door, his voice stopped and I knew he'd seen me. He was just staring at me with his mouth open. And I was looking at him and it seemed like all the air had been sucked óut of the sanctuary. I could feel everyone shifting in their pews, looking back and forth between us, but we were just locked on each other's eyes and time had stopped.

"Finally he said, 'Excuse me, folks, my son is here,' and everybody turned around in their pews to look at me and since they hadn't seen me in a while, they started clapping and he stepped down from the pulpit and I walked down the aisle and we hugged each other right there in the middle of church! He started crying. Then I started crying. Then everybody else started crying. It was a crazy thing."

"What happened?"

"Well, while he was hugging me, he whispered in my ear, 'I missed you,' and I whispered back, 'I love you, Dad.' And, after a second, he went back up to the pulpit and continued his sermon about the movie and redemption, and I think he threw in a bit about the prodigal son returning, and it was just amazing."

"And you and your dad?" I asked.

"It's been great. I'm still not sure how I feel about organized religion, but he knows where I stand and I know where he stands and it's okay. Occasionally he tries to get me back in the fold--more often as he's gotten older." He laughs to himself. "But, what can I do? I mean, that's his *job*."

CORN

"If only the world were as simple as baseball in a cornfield."
- 2004 guestbook entry, *Field of Dreams* movie site

I spent the first few days at the movie location having a variety of "candid" photographs taken of my character, John, to accompany Ray's monologue at the beginning of the film. Only six of these photos ended up in the movie, but we shot at least a dozen more, so that Phil and the editor, Ian Crafford, would have plenty to choose from in the editing room.

Melinda Sue Gordon was the still photographer for *Shoeless Joe*. Shy and sweet, she would walk around quietly in her wide brimmed hat, shooting photographs of the cast and crew making the movie. For the next few days, she had the additional responsibility of trying to tell John Kinsella's backstory in pictures.

These little photo shoots were fun, as each one of them was like shooting a mini-movie in an hour, from selecting a location, to finding the right wardrobe, to re-styling or graying my hair to show an age progression, and finally, to deciding on just the right pose to convey the gradual hardening of a man due to hard work, a rough life and the slow deterioration of his dreams.

In addition to her uncanny ability to be "invisible" on a busy set, Melinda Sue is also very smart and funny and I had a good time trying to make her laugh while she made sure everything was perfect for her photos.

For the most part, Melinda Sue shot these photos in sequence and so we started with shots of a young teenaged John standing next to a cornfield in overalls and a smile, holding an ear of corn proudly as if he had invented it. None of these ended up in the movie. Instead, they used a photo of a younger boy as John, sitting in a field.

We were forced to shoot these corn photos in the rows closest to the little creek that ran through the farm because, due to its proximity to the water, the corn there was the tallest.

As a young man growing up on a farm, when my father didn't have us downstairs digging in the basement, we were up in our one-acre garden, weeding rows of vegetables. With Grandaddy's intense supervision, I learned early how to hoe the weeds effectively out of a row of corn.

Even without this early experience in gardening, I think anyone could see there was something wrong with the corn in Iowa in the summer of '88. I had just had my photos taken next to corn that was seven feet tall, but by looking down the rows, I could see that not even fifty feet away, the corn was still only waist high.

"Looks pretty funny, don't it?" I jumped. Don Lansing had a way of appearing next to you without a sound. Some of the crew had a theory that he had secret tunnels hidden all over the farm to facilitate his silent appearances whenever he was least expected.

"Yeah, why is the corn so short?"

"No rain. Just won't grow. Worst drought since the Dust Bowl, everybody's sayin." Don spoke in short clips, like they were charging him extra for pronouns. Then he'd look you in the eye for a second to make sure you were following.

"What happened to this stuff?" I pointed to the tall stalks next to us.

"Watered it. Told me it was gonna look pretty funny if them ball-players come walkin' outta corn that's not even as tall as their white socks." His grin burst out. "They come to me, askin' if I'd mind if they dammed up the creek. I said 'No, you go right ahead.' Then they ask me, do I 'got a giant sprinkler head or somethin?' All I got is this big manure spreader, kinda looks like a big, ole rainbird. So, sure enough they hook it up, put the intake hose into the reservoir they made and start pumpin'. In this kinda heat, it's like a greenhouse. The corn's been growin' like crazy. My neighbors ain't too happy about it..."

"But, what about the short stuff out there?" I pointed down the rows. "Are they going to water that, too?"

"Say it don't matter. Camera will think it's smaller 'cuz it's in the distance."

"Well, I guess you're a pretty lucky guy—you rent your farm and you get your corn watered."

"Yeah, and totally fixed up my house. Put in new windows, hard-wood floors, even made the porch bigger, it's beautiful." He smiles conspiratorially. "Even got free air-conditioning. Not bad for a 90 year-old house."

The film company was learning that being on a farm brings out an innovative survival instinct in people. When you have to depend on the land and the weather for your sustenance (or to complete a movie), ingenuity tends to grow like a weed.

Besides damming the creek to irrigate, executive producer Brian Frankish had also taken the clever precaution of "insuring" the corn, as if it were an actor in the film. Frequently, movie production companies take insurance policies out on their star actors to avoid a disastrous loss if that star is unable to perform for a period of time due to injury or "personal problems."

When he contacted the claims adjuster about the drought-stricken corn, the company was more than happy to pay for the irrigation and the lost shooting days, rather than having to pay the full benefit of a $3 million policy.

But, just in case, production designer Dennis Gassner had placed an order for 60,000 life-sized corn stalks made out of silk from a company in Korea.

In the end, the corn-watering program worked. In fact, it worked a little too well. When they finally shot Kevin walking through the corn to hear the Voice, the stalks were over seven feet high and Kevin (who is 6'1") couldn't be seen between the rows of towering corn. A narrow, raised platform had to be built between the rows for Kevin to walk on to accommodate the filming.

Before my father moved our family, he had never farmed before in his life. But after the success of our first summer vegetable garden on the farm when I was ten years old, he had a brainstorm.

He decided to form a little family company that would "invest" in our garden in the spring by buying seeds and then reap the benefits in the fall by "selling" the vegetables to my mother, who would otherwise be paying for them at the local grocery store.

To us kids, this farm idea just sounded like more work. When he added that one of the benefits of forming this company would be that, as employees, we would be paid for our work planting and weeding in the garden, the tide of dissent changed immediately.

We agreed to give it a try.

At the first meeting, we discussed names for the new endeavor and held elections for the company officers. With a president, a secretary, and a treasurer, there were only my parents left to be the members-at-large. Monthly business meetings would be conducted using Robert's Rules of Order and officers would be re-elected once a year. We created by-laws and adopted a mission statement.

In the most contentious issue of the first meeting, it was decided that the new business would be called Fer-Ri-Bar Farm, using the first syllable of each of our names (as I've mentioned, my family called me Rick). My sister Barbara was not keen on taking third billing to her younger brothers, but alas, she was outvoted. (I had suggested "Barb-Dwier Farms," which I thought was a clever play on words that left my brother out entirely.) Barb was appeased by being elected the company's first president, encouraging her early fascination with business.

In order to raise capital to buy seeds in the spring, we would create shares of stock that we would offer to family and friends at an initial price of $1 a share. As treasurer, I was put in charge of creating an official-looking stock certificate using the Spirograph that I had been given for Christmas. Profits would be returned to investors in the form of dividends.

Monthly meetings were called to order, followed by a reading of the minutes, a treasurer's report, and old business followed by new business. Each motion had to be seconded, then discussed and finally voted upon.

As our only "customers," Mom and Dad chose what we would plant in the spring, and it was voted that workers would receive 3 cents for weeding a 100-foot row of corn or potatoes or beans or peas. It was Grandaddy's suggestion that we would also be required to pull off the soft, pink potato bugs and the hard, striped potato beetles and drop them into a tin can half-filled with kerosene. Most of Grandaddy's suggestions somehow involved the use of kerosene.

Row-weeding assignments were alternated by randomly picking row numbers at the beginning of each week and we were paid every two weeks.

Mom kept track of the harvest and paid the company the going price for the vegetables. At the end of the year, Fer-Ri-Bar Farm had turned a profit and offered a 20-cent-per-share dividend to its stockholders.

Based on the success of our first year in business, my father suggested we expand it. Noticing how much we enjoyed spending our hard-earned weeding money on penny candy at the local Ben Franklin store, he suggested that Fer-Ri-Bar find a wholesale source for penny candy and sell it back to us at a company store, creating a profit for stockholders, i.e., us. Between "Uncles" and "Aunts" who were just friends of my father's, and Uncle Bill and our cousins, there were over a hundred shares in circulation. Our rich Uncle Buster wasn't interested.

Needless to say, the motion to create a candy store in our own house passed unanimously, without much discussion. We found a wholesale candy distributor in nearby Medina, Ohio, and started out buying a box of 144 Atomic Fireballs for 88 cents.

We set up the store in the new, still-unpainted pantry my father had built while remodeling the kitchen and the dining room. A yellowed Tupperware container served as the cashbox and all store business was conducted on the honor system.

The store sold out in record time and the red-tongued board members voted *en blocke* to expand Fer-Ri-Bar's new sideline candy business. Soon, licorice nibs (3 for a penny) and pretzel sticks (10 cents a box—my suggestion) paved the way for Pixie-stix, Smarties, malted milk balls (my dad's favorite), boxes of Good-n-Plenty and pic-a-pop sodas in dozens of flavors. Business was booming, dividends were flowing and the few neighbor kids who lived close enough were both confused and excited to buy candy at the Fer-Ri-Bar store in our pantry.

Several stock splits happened in the first few years of business, and happy investors doubled-down their profits in more shares.

Somehow, my father had managed to teach us balance sheets, the stock market, corporate board operations, wholesale buying and Robert's Rules of Order, all while making a game out of it. A profitable one, too. Our cousins still joke about it being the best stock they ever bought. After several stock splits and overwhelming dividends, Fer-Ri-Bar Farm disbanded when the first of its board members went off to college, buying shares back at twice the original offering price, a whopping 2 dollars a share.

THE AUDITION

*"JOHN KINSELLA: (early-mid 20's) Serious, handsome, charismatic, magical young
man with clear wisdom beyond his years. One look in his eyes and it's clear that he is a
very special, old soul."*
- Casting breakdown for *Shoeless Joe*

N on-celebrity actors spend their whole lives doing one of the most
humbling acts on the planet—trying to get a job. And good
roles are hard to find. I had read the novel a few years earlier,
so as soon as my agent read me the character description from the casting
breakdown for *Shoeless Joe*, I was determined to get the part. Unfortunately,
there were hundreds of other actors with the same idea.

My audition was set for 1:10 p.m. on Monday, March 28, 1988.
One week before the audition, I re-read the book. I studied the audition
"sides," which were the last five pages of the script. It was a magical scene.
The opportunities to audition for movies this sweet and inspiring didn't
come along very often.

When it comes to an audition, wanting the job too much can work
against you. The director can sense your desperation. It helps if you can
channel your desire into the role so it looks like it's the character's desire
to get what he needs in the scene and not the actor's desire to get the role.

What does John Kinsella want? To make peace with his son. To be
forgiven for his sins as a father. To let Ray know he loves him. Without
ever actually saying it. *This would be a challenge.*

On the day of the audition, I arrived at the casting office, a nondescript stucco building directly adjacent to the busy Hollywood Freeway. I made my way to the office and put my name on the sign-in sheet. I saw Jim Carrey's name on the sheet from earlier in the day. Usually I make a concerted effort not to look at other names on the sign-in sheet to avoid getting intimidated, but there it was.

I began to feel the nerves tightening my chest and neck. There were several other actors waiting who, like me, looked enough like Kevin Costner to play his father. They were sitting in chairs, studying their scripts and mumbling the lines to themselves.

I tried to calm myself down. *If I am meant to play this role, I will play it. I have done my homework. I am ready.*

Eventually, my name was called. I let go of all of my preparation, and trusted that it would be there when I needed it. *I am John Kinsella...*

I entered the office like I was walking out of the corn onto a perfect baseball field...

The moments immediately after an audition tend to be ones of either elation or depression. I relive every moment of the session in my mind to evaluate it for small successes or failures. *Did I keep the pace up? Did I stumble on my lines? Was I convincing? Did she like me?*

Auditioning can be a little like trying to hit a baseball. You have to practice your swing and try to perfect your mechanics before you step to the plate, but once you get there, it's a dance. You have to let it all go and be ready to use what the pitcher gives you.

Sometimes you get a hit; sometimes you go down swinging. Sometimes you deserve what you get; sometimes you get lucky. Over the years, I'm not sure my audition average is much higher than my batting average was for that sad season of Little League, but I learned from that season that you have to let go of your disappointment or you will carry it back to the plate with you.

As with batting, the less I remember about the audition, the more likely it is that I will get the role. If some part of my brain remembers what happened while I was reading, then my mind wasn't fully in the mind of the character I was playing. This is a frustrating phenomenon when I try to evaluate my audition. If I think it went well because I remember all the "perfect" things I did in the audition, I know I'm in trouble.

In the case of the *Shoeless Joe* audition, I hardly remembered a thing.

An actor's life is built on hope. Hope that you'll be good, hope that you'll get the part, hope that *this* will be the role that will skyrocket you to stardom. An actor's life can also be a waiting game. It is best when your agent calls to tell you that you got the part while you are still driving home from the audition. But that is rarely the case.

Offering an actor a role frequently requires agreement by a significant number of people, including the director, producers, casting director, studio or network executives. Sometimes you may be their first choice, but they continue to audition other people. Sometimes an established actor agrees to do a smaller part than usual and swoops in to take the role you've already won. In general, the longer it takes to hear about a particular role you've auditioned for, the smaller your chances are of getting it.

The days after my *Shoeless Joe* audition dragged by. I tried to go on with the usual activities of my life, but I made an effort to stay close to my phone (this was back in days before cell phones). Every ring brought a rush of adrenaline to my chest, only to end in disappointment. As the weeks passed, my hope faded.

One Friday, the phone rang as I was preparing to get out of L.A. to go camping. I barely got to it before my message machine picked up. It was my agent. "Dwier, I have some good news…" It had been so long, I had almost forgotten about the audition. The six-week wait made the news even sweeter. I couldn't believe it! I was going to Iowa!

In addition to the thrill of having a job and the quality of the script, I had heard rumors that Jimmy Stewart was going to play Doc Graham.

I couldn't believe my good luck. I had grown up watching Mr. Stewart's films and had spent considerable time trying to imitate him in our bathroom mirror. His success in an industry dominated by bad boys always gave me hope that there was a place for nice guys in Hollywood.

I had come close to meeting Mr. Stewart before. My second job in Hollywood was a live national broadcast of Carson McCuller's play, *A Member of the Wedding*, with Pearl Bailey. It was directed by an Oscar-winning director who had worked in the early days of live television, and one of the nicest men around, Delbert Mann. I had learned from talking with him that he and his wife, Ann, were very good friends with Mr. Stewart and his wife, Gloria, and that the Stewarts were considering coming to opening night.

As the broadcast night approached, I began to feel the immense pressure of acting on live television, where any flubbed line or stumble would not only be seen by the 2,000 people in the theater audience in Nashville, but would also be immediately broadcast on CBS to 3 million viewers across the country. There would be no do-over or "Take two." On top of this, I made myself extra nervous, imagining that Jimmy Stewart would show up on opening night.

Despite my nervousness, I didn't flub my lines or fall off of the stage. The live broadcast of the play was a success and, for me, a thrilling throwback to a bygone era of television.

Mr. Stewart didn't end up coming to the theater that night but, I couldn't help but wonder if he sat at home in Hollywood watching *me* on television.

By the time I arrived on the set in Iowa, I had heard that health problems had prevented Mr. Stewart from accepting the role of Doc Graham. It was a disappointment to miss out on my second chance to meet him, but I hadn't given up hope.

Field of Dreams producers Larry and Chuck Gordon were young when their father died. Larry was eighteen and Chuck, only eleven. George Gordon had never seen his sons' success in show business. Larry was president of Twentieth Century Fox Studios when the script *Shoeless Joe* came across his desk. He immediately bought the rights, agreeing to let writer Phil Robinson direct the film. The Gordons hoped that making the movie would ease the pain of having lost their father so young.

After *Shoeless Joe* languished for four years at Fox, a shake-up at the studio allowed the Gordon brothers to open their own production company. As part of his departure deal, Larry took the script with him. He and his brother shopped the script at every studio, but no one was interested in making a baseball movie on a farm with ghosts.

Finally, Tom Pollock at Universal gave the picture the green light based on the fact that all of the execs who had read the script the night before the pitch meeting sheepishly admitted that they had ended up in tears by the final pages.

Kevin Costner had been at the top of their wish list to star in the movie but he had just finished filming *Bull Durham* and everyone was convinced he would not commit to another baseball movie. By chance, Universal executive Josh Donen ran into Costner at a restaurant and slipped him the script.

A week later, they got word that Costner wanted to do the movie. The Universal execs, along with Robinson and the Gordons, were ecstatic and they inked the deal. But *Bull Durham's* successful release was almost a year away and baseball movies were still a Hollywood pariah.

PERFECT

"Wonder, rather than doubt, is the root of knowledge."

- Abraham Joshua Heschel

I f there was ever a perfect moment with my father during my childhood, it was in the creek down at "The Country." The Country was my Grandaddy's summer cottage on 46 acres of remote, hilly land on a creek outside Richmond, Ohio, near the West Virginia border. There was no indoor toilet in the tiny house and we had to pump our water from a handpump in the yard. We would spend a week of my father's vacation every summer exploring nature, playing catch, sleeping on the porch and splashing in the creek.

In the water, my father turned into a child again. As if his dreams had been dehydrated, when he added water they became whole again. He relaxed in the water, he played in the water, he was fun in the water. We caught crayfish, we built dams and he taught us how to float on our backs.

The rocks in the creekbed could be hard and slippery, so before we ran down to the creek, we would clamber up the steep, narrow stairs to the stuffy attic, thick with hot air and the smell of mothballs. There, we would pull four or five large cardboard boxes from under the beds and rummage through to find a pair of "creek shoes." These were old, discarded shoes of all sizes, from children's to adults', from high top sneakers to leather dress shoes, all of them crispy from having been worn in the creek and then dried in the sun before being stashed again in the box under the beds.

Some were so hard and misshapen that we could barely get them onto our feet, but while we were running down to the water, the hardened leather would slowly surrender. Once the leather shoes spent a minute in the water, they would become pliant and vaguely slimy inside.

While we ran for the creek, Dad would cut a path with the riding lawnmower through the deep grass and raspberry brambles. It was slow going in the deep grass and the lawnmower engine would strain and complain as the deck filled with grass. Dad would stop for a moment, until it regained its speed, the wet, mulched grass would spew like lava out from under the mowing deck, and he would move on.

He would leave a perfect, narrow path back to the house, one that smelled of grass-times-a-thousand, one that was so verdant you could already feel everything growing back as soon as the spinning blades passed over like a perfect tornado.

After his labors on the mower, Dad would join us in the creek. He would do all of his old shtick: floating on his back and pretending his legs were shrinking by slowly bringing his knees to his chest, squirting water through his fist and always winning splash fights with the well-practiced hydrodynamic curve of his hands.

We would play games of "Marco Polo" in the shallow creek and then spend mindless hours building the rock dam to deepen the swimming hole. We would dry ourselves off on the threadbare "creek towels" and walk shivering through the evening air on the perfect path of fresh-cut grass to the warmth of the cottage.

The water would squish out of our sodden creek shoes as we walked, collecting bits of the freshly-mown grass on the way. We'd leave the wet, grass-covered shoes by the front porch to dry and make our way inside to warm up by the kerosene stove.

Bedtime would find us running from the warm stove to our sleeping bags, waiting for us on army cots on the screened-in porch, anticipating the final exhilaration of the cold flannel on our warm skin and the seamless transition to the last words of the day, spoken in the dark to a chorus of frogs. Then the deep, deep sleep.

Once we finished shooting the photos by the corn, Melinda Sue sent me to my trailer dressing room to make a wardrobe change.

A classic wedding photo was next. The actress they cast to play my wife was a a delightful girl from Cedar Rapids named Monica Baber. She had beautiful red hair and a quick laugh, and because she had also been hired as Amy Madigan's stand-in, she had already been on the set for over a month. They grayed my hair a bit at the temples and gave me some wrinkles and we laughed our way through our wedding photo and the little staged "picnic" until Melinda Sue was sure she had the perfect shots for the montage.

The other photos were intended to illustrate John's rapid aging and decline after Ray's mother died. We shot those in front of a green screen, so the appropriate background could be inserted later.

In one, a cute little boy was hired to be the young Ray as we pretended to pose in front of Ebbett's Field before a Yankee's game. In another, the make-up department gave me more gray hair and wrinkles for a photo of a weary John posing in front of a shipyard.

When the final photo was taken for the day, I walked across the back yard toward the makeup trailer. The sun was setting. The heat of the day was finally surrendering and a warm glow filled the sky. Magic hour.

Even though it had been a fun day and all I had been asked to do was stand in front of a camera, I was tired. I felt as if, mirroring the pictures I had just taken, I had lived an entire life in a day—growing up on a farm, getting married, having a son, working, getting old. In particular, the photos I had taken with the boy playing young Ray had made me wonder if I would ever have children of my own.

Playing with my brother's young sons, Justin and Nathan, was easy and fun, but what worried me was parenting a teenager. I had had such a hard time navigating my own teen years, and been so hard on my father during them, that I didn't want to feel responsible for guiding any of my own children through them.

My father was secretive about things that made no sense to me. He would say, "Don't tell the neighbors how much money I make."

"But I don't know how much money you make."

"Good, so you can't tell them." I thought about that for a second.

"How much money do you make?"

"Don't ask."

As a young teen, I began to notice that my father was not comfortable talking about anything other than work. He was certainly not comfortable talking about bodily functions. I was embarrassed that all of our family names for private parts and functions remained painfully juvenile, long after we grew up. Words like "wee-wee" and "bum-bum" were bad enough for small children, but it felt ridiculous to say them as a teenager.

When my brother was deemed old enough to hear about "the birds and the bees," we were both taken for a drive in the car, and vaguely told the facts of life. Being younger by fourteen months, I sat in the back seat of the station wagon, while Ferris sat in the front seat looking straight ahead and listening to my father's sterile and non-specific speech about the magic of reproduction.

In retrospect, it is clear my father did not want to have this awkward talk twice and figured he could lump me in a little early. The fourteen months difference between my brother's age and mine may as well have been a hundred years at this point in our development. Although I could see my brother occasionally nodding sheepishly in the front seat, I had no idea what they were talking about.

Dad ended with, "Oh, one more thing. Don't ever go to bed with a girl unless you're willing to marry her." At the time, "going to bed" meant "sleeping" to me, and the fear that I might accidently fall asleep anywhere near some girl that I didn't like remained a powerful insomniac for me for several months to follow.

My discomfort around girls lasted well into high school. I blamed my father for this social ineptitude.

Years later, when I did begin to have sex, many a romantic moment was ruined by my father's question in my head, "Am I really willing to marry this girl?"

When I arrived at the trailer to have my makeup removed, no one was there. I climbed up the steps and saw in the mirror what appeared to be my father walking toward me. I leaned in and looked. I had never thought of myself as looking like my father, but with a few drawn-on wrinkles and some gray hair, there was Dad. He looked back at me, inscrutable as always. I could see his face, but I still felt nothing about his death. *What was wrong with me?*

My father was not an expressive person. I had never seen him cry. When he laughed, it was always at the corniest of jokes. In addition to his lack of emotional expression, he was also very guarded talking about his family. He would frequently say that "family is the most important thing," and "you'll have your family for the rest of your life," but he never talked about his father, and never answered our questions about his eldest brother, our Uncle Buster, who, although from the same humble beginnings, had somehow become a multimillionaire. It was frustrating to me as a child to sense these secrets but not know why they were forbidden topics.

Dad would hold us to his stoic standards. "If you don't have anything nice to say about someone, don't say anything at all," were my father's watchwords. "Don't cry or I'll give you something to cry about," was usually enough of a warning from him to stifle our tears, and expressing anger directly was simply out of the question. He would never beat us. Spankings, when deserved, occurred only after calm deliberation.

My father tried hard to practice what he preached. But if he pinched his hand or hit his head while we were working, or if a tool he was using failed to do what it was supposed to do, he would occasionally burst into short cursing explosions.

If we happened to be working near him, we would simply keep our heads down, try not to make eye contact, and wait for the storm to pass. My mother would sigh and walk away and, later, my father would usually sit us down and apologize for his outburst.

As a result, without anyone saying it, we knew that expressing feelings was off limits in our house. No one cried or got angry, but we children all tried hard to make our parents laugh. It was understood that we all loved each other, but we never said the words "I love you." We didn't hug each other. Neither of my parents had grown up in households where such feelings were expressed openly and, therefore, neither did we.

The problem for me was that, as a young teenager, I was having a lot of feelings inside, but I had no place to let them out. I was angry about the hypocritical behavior I saw in the teachers at school and the elders at church. I was confused by the unfairness that randomly caused people to be born with physical or mental disabilities. I resented my grandaddy's bigoted worldview. I was angry that I had to work so much on my father's house.

Sometimes, if I was digging alone in the basement when I wanted to be playing outside, my frustration would get so overwhelming I wanted to scream. I imagined my full-throated voice ringing in my ears as I screamed uncontrollably in the dim basement, and the sound being deadened by the dirt walls around me.

But I knew that such a display would be simply unacceptable to my father. Instead, I would set the shovel aside and quietly punch the dirt walls as hard as I could until my anger was spent. The cool dirt felt good on my knuckles and "gave" just enough to be satisfying. Then I would pick up the shovel with my throbbing hands and numbly continue my work.

It was one of the reasons I played sports year-round. Playing fields aren't always a good place to vent emotions, either, but the intense physical exertion can help dissipate pent-up feelings. Anybody who has played high school football knows how good it feels to knock a linebacker onto his back.

My brother and sister didn't seem to share my volatile inner life. We all three got good grades and went to church every Sunday. We were polite and respectful and fun-loving. It felt like it was only *me* who had this hidden streak of discontent and frustration.

The summer before he started high school, my enterprising brother founded the Sharon Center Youth Theater in our little town of 300 people. He picked a couple of one-act plays from the Samuel French catalogue and my sister and I joined him and some friends to perform them. At first, it was a reprieve from work and I did it mostly for laughs, but I soon found a valuable fringe benefit. I began to enjoy pretending to be someone else, someone different from me, someone who was allowed to express his feelings.

I always wanted to play the villain in our summer melodramas, characters with names like Craven Sinclair and Munro Murgatroyd. I can still remember playing an angry Irish newspaperman, named Terry O'Dwyer (coincidentally), when I was thirteen, and screaming stereotypically; "Well, I'll be an orange-hearted Northern Irish if you're not the clumsiest oafareen!"

At first, it was forced and overdone, but the more I "pretended" to express my feelings, the more it became an effective release valve for what was really going on inside me. I could yell and cry and stomp around on-stage as someone else and my emotion was acceptable. In fact, the better I got at it, the more the audience would applaud me for expressing myself, instead of being told to keep it inside. This was a revelation to me.

"Were you in *Field of Dreams?* The movie?" he said softly.

"Yes, I was," I whispered back.

"The father, right?"

"That's right." He keeps staring at me in the bright lights of the library.

"You've got a good memory," I say to cover the awkward silence before I know what else to say. So far he hasn't said he liked the movie, or me *in* the movie, so I can't exactly say "Thank you."

"You're not as good-looking as you used to be."

Now I'm really on my heels. Do I say, "I'm sorry," or "Neither are you, probably?" While I decide, he says,

"You used to be really good-looking."

"Thank you." (I think?) I can see that this encounter is not going to be easy. I close the book I had been reading.

"My dad was an asshole." His words are perfectly formed, and he spits them out in short bursts.

"Oh."

He looks at the floor, contemplating this.

"I'm sorry," I say again.

"It's okay. It wasn't his fault." He looks up at me. "I'm an asshole, too."

Is he joking? Crazy? I laugh. It bursts out of me, forbidden, like I'm a kid in church. This is not what I expected from a stranger in a library. "I'm sorry," I say.

"No, it's okay. Like father, like son, right?"

I nod.

"He was just so quiet. I could never tell what he was thinking. He would try to do fatherly things with me: fishing, playing catch, target-shooting—I didn't like those things. I'd sit in that rowboat with my big, fat, orange lifejacket on, looking at the disgusting jar of worms he'd made me help him dig, and I would just be soooo bored, I would start talking. Talking and talking. Asking questions, singing songs, talking about movies. Just drove him crazy. 'You'll scare the fish,' he'd say." He did a deep-voiced monotone for his father's voice. I laughed.

"I wanted to scare the fish." His hands moved as quickly as his mouth did when he talked. "I didn't want to murder any fish."

"Well, he finally gave up. No more fishing trips, no more forced games of catch. I gave up, too. Just an uneasy silence between us. I grew up, moved out." He paused for a moment and tilted his head.

"Three years later, I get a call. It's my dad. He says he wants to take me to a movie. I say, 'Really?' I didn't know what was going on—I figured it was a trick, but I said 'Okay' anyway. But I didn't want to get stuck in a car with him, so he told me which theater and I met him there.

"When I saw it was *Field of Dreams,* I almost left. *A baseball movie?* I figured he was going to try to get me to play catch again or something. But I stayed anyway. Maybe I was in shock because I hadn't seen a movie with my dad since *The Sound of Music,* which we both loved, by the way—him for the Nazi-killing, me for the songs." I laughed again.

"To be honest, I had a little trouble getting into it at first. Corn, tractors...but I stuck it out. It was hard with Dad watching me out of the corner of his eye the whole time to see if I liked it. It gets to the end and the son says 'Hey Dad, you wanna have a catch?' and, I'll admit it, it got me a little bit. I'm a little teary and I look over and my dad, macho Sportsman of the Century, is crying his eyes out. I couldn't believe it!

My father never cried in his life.

"I couldn't help it. I put my arm around him. He's still crying and we watch the final shot together like a real father and son, maybe the closest moment we've ever spent together." He is pantomiming the moment, his arm around his imagined father.

"Suddenly I blurt out, 'Dad, I'm gay.' I said it straight to the screen, not even looking at him and I said it kinda loud because I didn't want to have to say it again. And I just waited. Sat there, with my arm ever-so-lightly on his shoulders, pretending to watch the credits and waiting for God-knows-what reaction from Dad.

"Looking back, I don't know why I said it right then. It was almost cruel. Maybe that's why I did it. I guess I figured I had my father as vulnerable as I'd ever seen him. If that cowboy could actually be crying, maybe he could also hear what I was trying to tell him.

"Out of the corner of my eye, I see that he's looking at the screen, too, and with his voice all hoarse, he says, 'I know that,' real matter-of-fact-like. 'Your mother told me. Why do you think I stopped takin' you fishin' and huntin'?'"

"'When I was thirteen? Why didn't you say something?'"

"'I didn't know what to say. It wasn't none of my business.'"

"'I'm your son, Dad. You could've told me that it was alright, that you loved me anyway.'"

"'I thought you knew that.' Dad looked surprised, like, *Of course I love you.* Then he said, 'Why do you think I took you fishin' and huntin'?'"

Da Boyz

"(late 20's – late 30's) Actors must be great baseball players. Whoring, boozing, high-spirited jocks. Locker-room characters. Note: Baseball players need not be perfect physical specimens. Slight paunch o.k., but not necessary."
-*Shoeless Joe* casting breakdown for the roles of the other banned baseball players: Happy Felsch, Buck Weaver, Eddie Cicotte and Swede Risberg.

They had looked for actor/ballplayers in New York, Dallas, Chicago and Atlanta before they decided to try looking in the "Show Biz Leagues" of industry recreational players, located right in North Hollywood.

Hundreds of guys were called in to read with casting director Margery Simkin. Twelve were invited to the baseball field at Hazeltine Park in North Hollywood to demonstrate their skills for Hall of Fame USC coach Rod Dedeaux and former Oriole Don Buford. If cast in the four roles, they would be taught to move more stiffly on the field in the style of 1920's ballplayers.

Chuck Hoyes from Philadelphia was fairly new to Hollywood and was desperate for a job. He chewed tobacco during his audition to help sell his look as a hard-boiled jock. He had played first base in high school and in college.

Unfortunately, Chuck had dislocated his shoulder in a Saturday industry league game and could hardly *move*, let alone participate in the callback. But his wife had just given birth to their first son and their bank account was nearly empty. He got three shots of novocaine in his shoulder before heading to the field.

Art Lafleur arrived at the tryout nursing a sore knee. He had played guard and linebacker at the University of Kentucky and had played softball in the industry leagues for years. When Rod Dedeaux told them to pick a position in the infield for some fielding drills, Art moved as quickly as he could to first base where he figured he would have the least chance of aggravating his already throbbing knee.

Art's stiff running and Chuck's shortened throwing motion were perfect to mimic the stiffer style of 20's era players. Chuck was cast as Swede Risberg and Art as Chick Gandil.

The day after the audition, Art's knee swelled up like a cantalope and further examination revealed he had a grade 3 tear in his meniscus. Fortunately, he had six weeks to nurse it before shooting started in Dyersville. In an effort to save a little money, Art cashed in his airline ticket to Iowa and instead drove his Jeep Cherokee. Before he left L.A., he tossed his set of horseshoes in the back of the car.

Steve Eastin (pitcher Eddie Cicotte), and Michael Mahurin (Buck Weaver), rounded out the main group of banned ballplayers. Long hours spent standing around in the hot Iowa sun in wool baseball uniforms bonded the four into an inseparable unit. Off screen, they jokingly pretended to be British noblemen and frequently spoke to each other in high-pitched English "fop" voices to crack each other up.

They set up horseshoe stakes and spent their off-camera time pitching shoes behind the barn, telling stories and jokes and pausing their game when the cameraman yelled "Rolling!" so as not to ruin a take with the clank of horseshoes.

The rest of the old-time ballplayers were cast from local semi-professional teams. A casting notice in the Dyersville area newspapers enticed over seventy men to the tryout; fifteen were cast in the movie and paid $50 a day. Several of those men went on to form The Ghost Players, a group of men who traveled the world playing old-time baseball for adoring fans.

As I was walking toward the barn to have my picture taken in a World War I army uniform on my second day at the farm location, I passed Phil Robinson walking toward the house. He was lost in thought. I wasn't sure if I should bother him. "How's it going?" I blurted.

"Oh, it's going…" He seemed different. Smaller. Although I was dressed in my crisp woolen army uniform, he seemed not to notice. "Did anyone tell you about the final scene?"

Oh my God, has the scene been cut? I thought to myself. "No, have there been changes?"

"I just wanted to tell you that John and I, John Lindley, the cinematographer and I…" He was hedging like he was notifying next of kin. "… we decided to shoot your scene at magic hour, só we'll have to break it up into smaller pieces."

"Oh, that's okay, I'll be ready." I felt like I was trying to cheer him up. I used to do that with my father when he would get that faraway look in his eyes, like he was lost in some pain I couldn't see. "I'm excited," I said. "I can't wait." He looked up at me like "excited" was an alien word.

"We might try to block it later, around sunset." (Blocking is a theatre term for rehearsing the actors' movements in a scene).

"Great. Good luck today." Phil walked toward the set slowly, savoring his last moments of solitude before the day's hard work began.

I arrived at the barn where Melinda Sue was already setting up the shot in a doorway. To the faint sound of clanging horseshoes, she took some pictures of me in the uniform that looked almost exactly like a photo I found years later of Granddaddy as a young man about to be shipped out to the war in Europe in 1917.

My grandfather, Fred Ferris, was from the same era as Shoeless Joe Jackson and his fellow players. He was a big man, particularly for his time. At 6' 4", 230 lbs., Grandaddy had played semi-professional football in 1913, when helmets were optional and teams would fill out their rosters with strong men from the local factories, like the ones in Steubenville, Ohio. I'd always heard that his picture is in the Football Hall of Fame with one such team, the Toronto Tigers. I imagine he played some baseball, too, but he never talked about it.

In his World War I infantry photo of the 332nd K Company, he is standing in the back row, soberly towering over his colleagues. His face doesn't tell you much—I know, I've studied it. I'd heard his stories of how K company, with its squadron of tall, strapping men, marched double-time, all over Italy, in an effort to make the Kaiser's army think the Americans had more troops there than they did, and that all of them were grim giants.

At home with us, my grandfather was a stern, silent man. He spoke softly and his speech was seasoned with odd rural pronunciations, such as calling "Cincinnati", "Cincinnatah" and saying "gangrene" like "ganjereen", as if it rhymed with "tangerine." When he did speak, it was usually about how he had gone to work when he was fourteen and how hard he had worked and, inevitably, about how little we had to work.

As teenagers, my brother and sister and I found this incredibly unfair. We were the hardest-working children we knew. While our friends were watching cartoons or playing miniature golf, almost every weekend found us digging in the basement, or tearing down a plaster wall, or weeding in the garden, or mowing the lawn, or cleaning the horses' stalls, or baling hay or pruning fruit trees. That he saw us as lazy confounded us.

My father always said, "If you can't say anything nice about someone, don't say anything at all." We didn't talk much about Grandaddy.

The only thing it was clear my grandfather loved was baseball. He would listen to ballgames while lying on his bed. I would sit outside his door in the living room and listen, too. The unique sound of a baseball game on the radio—the languid drawl of the announcers, the long pauses between pitches, the hypnotic static of the radio receiver—always lulls me to a sense of calm. If my grandfather was listening to a baseball game, then he wasn't scolding us for not working in the basement or in the garden, for not helping my dad more, or for killing our mother (his daughter), with our laziness.

The truth is, if anything was "killing" my mother, it was the fact that my grandfather had moved in with us. After my grandmother died of breast cancer when I was thirteen, there wasn't much for my retired grandfather to do. He didn't have many friends. The twelve siblings he had supported and helped raise didn't end up liking him very much. We understood why; he was not an easy man to live with.

He liked being with our family, because there was always work to do. Even in his late seventies, when he had slimmed to 190 pounds, his bony frame was awkward in a basement crawlspace being dug from its original five feet to a full eight-foot depth. But that did not deter him. He swung his pick-axe deftly and loosened large piles of dirt for us to load into the wagon and drag up the ramp. While we did, he would sit quietly on a camp stool, small beads of sweat soaking into the band of his railroad cap. After we'd unloaded the dirt and returned, he would slowly unfold his long legs like an underground spider, and calmly return to swinging his pick.

My brother and I always silently prayed that the old giant would tire out and go upstairs to rest, hoping that Dad might let us quit working for the day as well. It rarely happened. Quitting time usually came when dinner was ready, around 5 p.m.

Then, one day, as Grandaddy was packing for his annual winter drive to Florida, one of his Sunday dress shoes fell out of his hand and landed on his big toe. It was a minor accident and none of us would even have known about it, if it hadn't had such strange consequences.

After a month in Florida, Grandaddy called to tell my mom that he was going to the doctor because his foot was still swollen from that "little cut on his toe". The doctor saw that the infection had become gangrenous, and recommended that the leg be amputated as soon as possible. So, my mother flew immediately to Orlando and drove home two weeks later with her father, leaving his lower leg in Central Florida.

How strange that he had survived sixty years of hard labor in dangerous factories and marching around Italy during a World War, only to lose his leg to a dropped shoe.

If life with Grandaddy had been difficult before, it was exponentially worse after that. He was almost completely immobile and every doctor's appointment required a major troop movement. He was a big man and frequently needed two of us to help him stand up from or sit down on his bed. He had become as helpless as a baby and it fell to my mother to take care of him.

He had a bedpan that needed to be emptied several times a day, a "walker" that, as such a proud man, he was embarrassed to use, and a flesh-colored fiberglass leg, complete with a shoe on its artificial foot. I thought it ironic that this was the very shoe that had fallen on his foot and ultimately caused him to lose the leg.

Grandaddy's lack of mobility stepped up his baseball listening as well. He would lose himself in a baseball game, drifting in and out of sleep, trying to forget the ghost pains in his missing leg. Occasionally, he would make a comment out loud about the game, using racist words for players of color and punctuating any outstanding play by African-American players with, "He must be a half-breed..."

We were all embarrassed by my grandfather's racism. My mother would roll her eyes or scold him with an exasperated, "Dad!" as she fluffed his pillow to make him more comfortable. As I got older, his narrow-minded words made me increasingly angry and I was embarrassed that I was too afraid of him to say anything about it.

That was fine with him, because among his favorite sayings was, "Children should be seen and not heard." For years, I continued to listen to baseball games "with" him—Grandaddy in his room and I, unheard, on the living room couch outside his door.

EAST DUBUQUE

"Nobody could hit like Shoeless Joe."
- W. P. Kinsella

By the time I arrived in Iowa, the crew was getting restless. Most of them were Angelenos, far from friends and family and unaccustomed to the slower pace of life on a farm. As a result, many of the crewmembers found creative ways to keep themselves from going stir-crazy.

The art department created more souvenir *Shoeless Joe* t-shirts, jackets and caps for the cast and crew than I have ever seen on a movie production. The crew started a bowling team at the local lanes, complete with cool, vintage shirts with bowling aliases embroidered above the pocket on the front and "*Shoeless Joe* Bowling Team" on the back. I chose to be "Lou."

In addition to bowling nights, there were trips to the local dog track in Dubuque. I had never seen dog races before and the general seediness of the track itself was easy to ignore after a few drinks in the company of twenty fun-loving cast and crew members. Amy Madigan, who played Kevin's wife Annie in the movie, has an infectious laugh and Tim Busfield (Annie's practical brother Mark), is one of the funniest guys I've ever met.

Kevin Costner's hit movie, *Bull Durham*, was released in June of 1988 while he was shooting *Shoeless Joe* in Dyersville. Kevin rarely came out carousing with us, but when he did, he would quickly be surrounded by delighted fans. He was always gracious and I was envious to watch the frenzy that his growing stardom had created around him.

We were all flush with "per diem" money provided by the film company for meals and living expenses in Iowa. Per diem always feels like free money on a shoot (for me, it was $42 in cash each day) and a lot of it was left at the track.

When we weren't bowling or betting, there were frequent late-night trips across the river to East Dubuque for a few drinks. East Dubuque is one of many small towns popularized during Prohibition as a respite from the dry saloons and temperance leagues in Iowa. These towns were effectively exempt from Prohibition laws simply by being located just across the Mississippi River in "Capone Country."

East Dubuque is still known for its lineup of bars on Sinsinawa Street which stay open hours later than their counterparts in Iowa, and the restless *Shoeless Joe* cast and crew investigated many of them. Mulgrew's (formerly Toots'), Diamond Jim's and the Kat's Meow give way to joints with more generic names like Night Club, The Cave, Hang Out, The Other Side and Finally R Place. In fact, the only building on Sinsinawa Street that is not a bar or nightclub is the East Dubuque Police Department.

The relationship of Dubuque, Iowa to East Dubuque, Illnois reminded me of my early teen years. By the time I reached high school, because my sister and brother were such model students and goody two-shoes, I decided the only way to stand out in my family was to be rebellious.

Although I had been a wholesome, nerdy type like my siblings through most of my school career, in high school I began to cultivate a reputation amongst my classmates as a smart aleck. I prided myself on being able to say subversive comments at the perfect decibel level; loud enough to make everyone crack up around me, but not quite loud enough to be heard by the teacher. It was the beginning of my own life of secrets:

posing as the smart, innocent kid with good grades but living a secret life as a troublemaker.

When I was fourteen, I stole a deck of playing cards with photos of topless women on them: 52 different naked women in cheesy poses, looking provocatively at the camera. I hid them in a secret gap that had been accidently left in the drywall when my father was building my closet.

Frustrated by my father's unwillingness to express his feelings and reveal the truth about his family secrets, I began to lie to him. I would steal candy from our Fer-Ri-Bar Farm pantry store and, when cornered, I would lie about it. Sometimes I would lie about where I was or what I was doing. Sometimes I would lie about whether I was drinking, a habit that became more and more prevalent as I got older.

But sometimes I lied about things that he didn't even care about. Lying became a way for me to exert power over my father, and once I told a lie, I would never allow myself to admit to it. I would stick to my story, even in the light of overwhelming evidence to the contrary. There was a feeling of power in defending an indefensible lie, particularly if it was something that was difficult for him to refute.

Once, I skipped school to play pool and "get some Vitamin C" (code for vodka and orange juice) at a friend's house and, when caught, I told my father I had been studying at another friend's house.

"I know you're lying. I spoke to Mrs. Malek," my father said with growing impatience.

"Who are you going to believe: her or me?" I would challenge.

Looking back now, I can see I was trying to chip away at the block of granite that was my dad in order to see what was inside. It must have been extremely frustrating for him, having felt like he had done everything right, to be faced with such defiance and impertinence.

The last time my father spanked me, I was fifteen and really too old to be spanked. I knew it and he knew it, but we went through with it anyway. He started with his usual disclaimer, "This is going to hurt me more than it's going to hurt you."

"Then why bother?" I mumbled under my breath.

He pursed his lips as his neck turned red. On his command, I pulled down the back of my pants and laid awkwardly across his knees as he sat on the edge of my bed. I was a stick figure, a gangly teenager, inches taller than him, and all legs and arms, glaring upside down at my astronaut wallpaper.

He swatted me with his hand and, despite similar protestations in the past, this time it really didn't hurt me. Neither one of us had wanted it to go this far, but neither one of us could back down.

He had gotten his way, but some unspoken threshold had been crossed. He never tried to spank me again. He would have to find other ways to punish his wayward son.

HUGS TO OHIO

"My life is messy, so in art I can create order."

‑ Gregory Crewdson

Burt Lancaster, along with Jimmy Stewart, John Wayne and Humphrey Bogart, was one of the stars I tried to do imitations of when I was young. His breathy, laughing voice was fun to mimic and it always got a chuckle from my family and friends. So, meeting him on the set of *Field of Dreams* was a treat.

We never had a scene together in the movie, and his last few days on the set were my first few days, but I made a point to be around when his final scene was being shot. Because of the heat and Mr. Lancaster's commitment to another film shooting in Italy, Phil tried to get his work out of the way early in the day. Mr. Lancaster had been a little surly that day and everyone was tiptoeing around him.

I had a theory that because Mr. Lancaster had been such an athlete as a young man, (he had a basketball scholarship at NYU that he gave up to start an acrobatic act, which toured at circuses and in vaudeville), it was frustrating for him to see all the younger men playing baseball on the set, when his body was no longer able to.

When there was a pause between scenes, I took a chance and walked up to him. He was sitting alone in the shade in a tall director's chair with his name on the back. "Mr. Lancaster, my name's Dwier Brown and I just wanted to tell you that I'm a big fan of your work." He turned toward me with a scowl and I knew I had made a mistake. I prepared to apologize and retreat. He saw my pin-striped uniform and squinted up at me from his chair.

A smile opened his face. "Why, thank you." He put out his hand. "Burt Lanc'stah." He said his last name with his New York accent as if it were only one syllable. "What did you say your name was?" Hearing his sing-song voice in person for the first time felt like catching a rare butterfly. I had a sudden urge to answer the question in "his" voice. I shook his hand instead.

"I'm Dwier Brown. I play John Kinsella."

"Pleased to meet you, John Kinsella. I play Doc Graham." I stood there, nodding and smiling. I hadn't really prepared what to say next. "'Kinsella' is an Irish name, isn't it?" he said.

"That's what it says in the script."

"'Graham' is Scottish. They would pronounce it in two quick syllables: 'Gree-ham.' Did you know that?"

Just then, the assistant director came to usher him to the set. Doc Graham said to me, "Excuse me, please, John Kinsella." He walked toward the camera for his last shot of the film and, when he finished, he was driven away to the airport. *Field of Dreams* was the last film of Burt Lancaster's amazing career.

Although I had tried to impersonate my favorite movie stars when I was growing up, I had never known anyone who was a professional actor. When I told people that I was planning to take drama classes in college, they would inevitably ask, "But what are you going to do to make a *living*?" I didn't know the answer to that question.

As a carefree college student, I just knew that I liked being on stage, that my theater classes were the most challenging, creative ones I had, and that the other people doing these plays with me were the strangest, funniest people I had ever met.

In my quest to become a man as different from my stoic father and my bigoted grandfather as possible, one who was happy and communicative, one who could talk about something other than work, I subconsciously recruited a few surrogate fathers.

The head of the drama department at Ashland College was everything my father wasn't. Murray Hudson was a funny, fiery Irish-American actor with a quick wit and an easy charm. He inspired my performances onstage and then rewarded me with tearful tenor solos and drunken boxing lessons at the cast parties.

When graduation time came, even Murray, who liked me as much as I loved him, wouldn't give me any assurances that I could make a living as an actor. Like a good father, he knew that I might cling to his promises and expect the powers in show business to make good on them.

Without Murray's blessing, I came up with my own plan for my future success. I would use my marketing minor to get a job locally in advertising, maybe writing copy for radio commercials. I would then parlay my success as a copywriter into a similar job in New York City. Once I got settled in the Big Apple, I would start auditioning for plays until I could quit my day job and become a full-time actor.

It was a perfect plan for a Midwestern farmboy. It was cautious, yet optimistic. It would use the skills I had worked hard to achieve in college. It was responsible and would depend upon the kindness of strangers. It was, in short, ridiculously naïve.

But it was a plan. Even my practical parents pretended to see the thoughtful wisdom of it. My mother, who had always encouraged my artistic endeavors (from puppet shows to pantomime), was less enthusiastic about it than I hoped, but she had watched my older sister move to Paris and my brother move to Washington, D.C., and may have just been dreading her soon-to-be-empty nest.

It was my father's support that was most surprising. He advised me to give my dream of becoming an actor a chance for five years. If it wasn't working after the trial period, he insisted, it could be changed, like moving a wall in an old house. Perhaps because he had spent so much of his life making money in jobs that were tedious and unfulfilling, he was circumspect enough to offer his blessing on the kind of plan he had never had the luxury to pursue.

So, everything was set. All I needed to do was to get an entry-level job at an ad agency in the nearby bustling metropolis of Mansfield, Ohio (population 50,000) and, quick as a wink, I would be tap-dancing in the footlights of Broadway.

Unfortunately, the national economy was struggling and there were no jobs in advertising in central Ohio in the summer of 1980. After only three months, my five-year plan was stalled.

I decided to set off for Chicago to see if I could audition for the famous Second City improvisational comedy troupe. I had joined some friends doing improv gigs in college and had really enjoyed the rapid-fire fun of just making it up as we went along. We had even videotaped some of our scripted material and created a cable access TV show called *Accordion Repair.*

I figured if I was going to "starve" as an actor, I may as well do it when I was young and without a family to support. I took a train to Chicago in September of 1980 with $300 in my pocket.

Through the kindness of strangers, I found a place to sleep at the Evanston home of a couple, the McGill's, who were friends of friends. I managed to "act" my way into a job waiting tables at the Wrigley Building Restaurant in downtown Chicago by telling them I had restaurant experience. The truth was, I had only ever *eaten* in a restaurant a dozen times before, as dining out was reserved as a celebration for when my father got a raise at work. Needless to say, I did not have much skill as a waiter.

After struggling through my lunch shift and trying to learn on the job, I would eat as big a free meal as I could before I left. I would then audition for any show that I could find or try to muster the courage to walk in the door of one of Chicago's five main talent agents to introduce myself.

Once in the door, I would usually stand awkwardly in the corner of the waiting room, smiling and hoping the receptionist would notice me. I didn't want to be rude by bothering her. Sometimes I would leave only when the agency closed for the day and I would finally try to talk to the receptionist on the elevator on her way out of the building.

At night, I would usher at any theater that would let me see their show in exchange for handing out programs and helping patrons find their seats. Sometimes, after that, I would rush down to Wells Street to see the free late night improv set at Second City.

I learned quickly that theatre people are a "huggy" bunch. Hugging was new to me. My experience of hugging in Ohio only occurred in the direst of emergencies and usually started with a handshake. It would then morph awkwardly into an arm over the shoulder for gentle thumps on the back, the clenched handshake still squeezed between bodies with backs arched to avoid any possible contact below the waist.

Suddenly I found myself at the theater spending days and nights with the huggiest bunch of people I had ever known. We greeted each other at rehearsal with hugs and ended the day with more hugs. These were good hugs too, without a handshake stuffed in between for protection, and these with people I had only known for a few days.

That Christmas, when I took the train to visit my family for the holidays, I decided to institute a hugging program with my unsuspecting family. Part of my intention was to break the stoic chain my family had always been bound up with, but I'm sure another part was to show off the worldliness I had acquired in the Big City.

When I climbed off the train in Akron and walked across the snowy platform to meet my parents in the lobby, I headed straight for my mom and wrapped my arms around her. She hugged me back, but her rigid smile made me think she was grateful for the thick, winter coats we both were wearing. My father was smiling too, but when I brushed past his outstretched hand to embrace him, he froze with his one arm still waiting for a manly handshake and the other stiffly at his side. After a moment, I released him and he asked, "How was the train ride?"

"It was fine, Dad," I said, and we fell quickly back into small talk about the train and the weather. What is there about fathers and planes, trains, ships and automobiles? I've had friends whose fathers could only talk comfortably with them about their cars. "How's your car runnin'?" "Have you had the oil changed?" Fathers want to fix things, and cars can be fixed. Soft feelings and tender emotions are not so easily fixable. Better to avoid them.

On Christmas Eve, after everyone had finished wrapping their gifts, I asked the family to sit around what had been my grandfather's dining room table and nervously told them about my experiment. "I know we all love each other, but we never take the time to say it out loud or to hug each other. Up in Chicago, I'm hugging these people I barely even know and it made me realize that I don't even do that with my family. I know it may be a little weird at first but I'd like us all to try to be a little more expressive with each other, okay?"

There were casual shrugs of assent around the table, as if I had asked them nothing more than to rinse their dinner dishes before they put them in the sink. No one in our family made announcements at the dinner table, and everyone had been a little suspicious about what I wanted to talk to them about. But we had all been taught to be reasonable, rational people and what I was asking didn't seem too crazy. Awkward, maybe, but not unreasonable.

"When are we supposed to hug?" asked my brother.

"I don't know, anytime you feel like it," I replied. Nods all around.

"Well, what for?" my sister, ever the practical one, asked.

"It feels good, and it reminds us that we love each other." More nods. "Besides, you won't lie on your deathbed and wish you had spent more time hugging."

There was a long pause as I watched my family look around at each other with embarrassed grins on their faces like teens in a sexuality class. "Okay, do we try it now?" smirked my sister.

My brother laughed loudly, "In case we die in our sleep?"

"Sure, why not?" We all stood up and I walked halfway around Grandaddy's worn oak table and hugged my sister. She was still smiling sheepishly when I leaned in, like she was playing a game of Truth or Dare at a pajama party. She patted me gently on the shoulder as we embraced.

"Merry Christmas," she said and backed up stiffly before moving on to hug my brother, who had just set my mother back onto the ground after his crushing embrace.

I wrapped my arms around her and she tentatively slid her arms around me. "I love you, Mom."

"I love you too, honey." I was always amazed how willing and open my mother was to whatever crazy idea I happened to bring home.

My brother, who had been joking his way through these embraces, threw his arms under mine and squeezed, lifting me off the ground like it was a takedown move and laughing in my ear. Once he set me down, I hung onto him for an extra second before I let him go.

At the head of the table stood my father, whose discomfort was palpable. I stepped toward him and casually put my arms around him. His hands still hung limply at his sides. Through the faintest hint of his

Old Spice after-shave I said, "I love you, Dad," and lingered for a moment more.

"All right," he said.

I had been standing in line at a Dorchester deli, waiting for my sister, when he nudged me on the shoulder and said, 'Hey, you wanna have a catch?' When I turned, he laughed and told me how much he loved *Field of Dreams*.

"But my dad was a jehk." He covered his mouth. "Shoot! I'm nawt supposed to say that. I made a deal with my bruthah…" His Boston accent was thick, like the guys on the radio show, *Car Talk*. His voice was so loud that the other patrons were backing away from us, but I was still trying to lip-read so I could understand him. "I'm Bawbby." He put out his hand and laughed suddenly. "Mikey's gonna shit his pants that I met you… Right heah in Dawchistah!" I shook his hand.

"I'm Dwier."

"Dee-wah!?"

"Dwi-er."

"Oh, Duh-wi-ah. Plezshah ta meet ya." The guy was a little shorter than I was, but beefier, coiffed black hair, dark stubble and flecks of gray on his chin.

"I'm sorry. What deal did you make with your brother?" I tried talking softly in hopes that he could take a hint.

"Oh, my dad was an alcoholic! He drank a lawt. Pretty much chased my mowm away. It made my bruthah and me pretty scrappy guys. If things gawt hahd in our lives, we would just say 'This is nothing compared to what Dad put us through.' I managed to get out of the house when I was eighteen, took my little bruthah Mikey with me—I couldn't leave him. We nevah looked back.

"Dad died in '77 and it's kinda messed up 'cuz we nevah got a chance to have it out with him. Didn't think about him much either, until someone would talk about their dad. Then I would tell a story about my dad, how he hit us, or how my bruthah and I would hide from him down the cellah or stay at friends' houses until it was late enough that we knew he would be passed out.

"I gawt to enjoy tellin' those stories. It made me feel good about myself. It was like a badge of courage: 'I survived my fathah's abuse.' Girls loved 'em, too. Those abusive Dad stories got me laid sooo many times…" He laughs loudly. The woman behind him backed up.

"So, years later, I get married, Mike gets married, we both got boys of our own. But it's kinda weird 'cuz we don't know how to *be* dads, really. I mean, 'cuz our dad was such a mess. All we gawt are these abusive stories we've been hangin' on to and the trouble with telling those stories to othah people is then you staht telling 'em to your*self.*" He raised his dark eyebrows at me for emphasis. "Givin' yourself excuses, ya know what I mean?"

"I do." I planned to say more, but…

"The Spring of '88, my bruthah reads in the paypah about them needin' extras for a baseball movie they're shooting at Fenway called *Shoeless Joe.* We go to the stadium and it's wicked boring but—" he interrupts himself—"Hey, did you know Matt Damon and Ben Affleck weh theh, too? As extras?"

"I heard that but I wasn't sure it was true."

"Oh, it's true. For shuwah. You know, they're from Bawston, so…"

"*That* I knew."

"So, anyway, we weh in the stands for that and now my bruthah and I can say we acted in a movie with Kevin Cawstnah and James Eahl Jones and Matt Damon and Ben Affleck. And *you.* Pretty cool, huh?"

"Very cool." I noticed he mentioned *me* as an afterthought. I'd gotten used to it. Most people whose first question is, "Were you in *Field of Dreams?*"—their second question is, "What's Kevin like?"

"So, a year later, my bruthah calls me and says the movie we weh in came out but now it's called *Field of Dreams*. Kinda stupid name, I thought. But we go and it's a pissah, thinking we might see ahselves in the movie.

"Well, the Fenway scenes come up and we cheer, along with the other Sawx fans in the crowd, but we wuh just specks in the background, way out by the Monstah. Couldn't see anything of us. We wuh bummed, I think we yelled something at the screen like 'Wheh's our close-up?'" He laughs. "But we just kept watchin' the movie.

"At the end, the father comes in, and there *you* are, and the whole theatah is just dead quiet and I staht to hear people cryin' around me. Suddenly, I staht sweatin' and my eyes staht burning. It's really dark and I can feel my bruthah next to me and he's all tense and I'm tryin' to hold it togethah and he's tryin' to hold it togethah.

"Then Cawstnah says, 'Hey, Dad…' and all of a sudden, I hear Mike choke a little bit and I just fall apaht. I start cryin' like a freakin' baby and Mikey heahs me and he starts cryin' like a baby and I put my arm on his shoulder and we just cried our eyes out for five minutes, bawlin' and blubberin', snawt everywheh, holdin' each other and cryin'. I nevah seen Mike cry before, nawt since he was a kid and he'd neveh seen me, and we… we weh a mess.

"And I'm thinkin', 'Why are *we* cryin'? Our old man was a jehk!' So Mike and I sit theh for a long time. Finally we staggah out of the show and we're drivin' home. We started talkin' about Dad and those stories we told for so long about him abusin' us. Then we talked about him takin' us to Fenway when we weh little and what a crazy Sawx fan he was. And about how hahd it is to be a dad sometimes.

"Mike says, 'Dad was only a real asshole for a few years once we weh teenagers, but we been carryin' those stories around for years aftah. Re-livin''em and feelin' sorry for ourselves.'

"He said, 'What if we just let Dad off the hook, give him a mulligan, you know—a do-ovah, and for the sake of our boys, staht to remembah some of the othah stuff about him. We wah kinda assholes ourselves when we wah teenagers.' And he was right—we totally wah." He starts to laugh, then takes it back.

"I think it was a little harder for me 'cuz I was the older bruthah, tryin' to protect him back then..." He paused for a moment. "But then I thought, 'What the hell? Dad's dead now and I'm not always the best fathah either.'

"So me and Mike made this deal to try to remembah bettah stuff about him. Now sometimes we can laugh about stuff Dad did, stuff that we used to get all worked up about."

He looked down at his shoes and I saw that his stubbled chin was quivering. I put my hand on his shoulder. He turned his head away and inhaled shakily. "I'm sorry..." He wiped his face with his hand quickly so I wouldn't see it.

"That's okay." I stood in the bright deli, patting his shoulder. "It's okay..." The older woman in line behind him slowly moved away from us.

"I want to talk to 'im sometimes. Tell 'im we forgave him... Anyway..." He breathed deeply again. His face was tight. "Anyway, thanks for... thanks for being in that movie." His green eyes flashed up to mine, still brimming with tears.

With my hand on his shoulder, I started to pull him toward me and he crushed me like a long-lost relative. We stood there for a long time in the fluorescent lighting of the deli line.

When he finally let me go he said, "Next time you watch the movie, you look for us at Fenway." He laughed. "Hey! My bruthah is not gonna *believe* that I met you." He looked around us, wiping his face again. He turned back to me, "So, what's Cawstnah like?"

INDEPENDENCE DAY

"By trying, we can easily endure adversity, Another man's, I mean ."
- Mark Twain

I spent a few months acclimating myself to Chicago life, public transportation and restaurant work, while doing a few plays on the side. Finally, I got cast in my first professional acting job, in the summer company at the Organic Theater, newly housed in a warehouse on Clark St. It was a long way from being in a movie like *Field of Dreams*, but it was a start. It was a diverse group of younger actors mixing with the veteran company members, under the guidance of an eccentric, bearded, and bald genius named Stuart Gordon.

Hot off the success of their cult classic *Bleacher Bums*, the Organic Theater Company was a rag-tag bunch of misfits who created their own brand of theatre through improv and ingenious staging techniques. They had decided to start their 1981 season and the opening of their new "warehouse space" theater on Clark St. with an adaptation of Mary Renault's novel, *The King Must Die*.

Along with a group of their regular Equity actors, we summer interns began training in tumbling and acrobatics in order to actually perform Theseus' "bull-leaping" stunts on a real dirt floor they had created inside the theater. We would each play several roles in the production, including two of us under a stylized bull costume made out of black wrestling mat material, actually flipping other actors off the "head" of the bull, while charging somewhat blindly around the dirt arena.

This "style" of theatre was a trial by fire for a Midwestern farmboy accustomed to living room dramas performed on proscenium stages.

There were lightning fast costume changes and special effects and skimpy costumes and full-body make-up to give us all the dark skin of swarthy Greek kings and acrobats. I had been required to wear a Speedo bathing suit as a lifeguard for three summers in Ohio, but that was chaste compared to the loincloths we all wore in front of the audiences of *The King Must Die*.

Before the show, we interns (four men and four women) would use sponges to cover every visible inch of our bodies with a cold mixture of dark makeup and water stored in cut-off gallon milk jugs. Naturally, we would check each other carefully for missed spots before heading to the stage for our tumbling warm-up. I had always been a fan of the feminine form, but this new casual touching and familiarity was like walking into a *Playboy* spread of "Girls of the Greek Bull-leapers."

One of the beautiful, talented actresses in the cast was having trouble making a quick costume change from a peasant bull-leaper to her next entrance as the topless Queen Ariadne. There was a jeweled robe and a giant headdress to put on as well as elaborate make-up that consistently made her a few seconds late for her pivotal entrance. Because I had some down time in Act Two, she asked me to help her. I tried to act cool but I hoped the dark body make-up hid my blushing face.

For the run of the play, in the second act, I could be found backstage on my knees carefully painting gold make-up onto the actress's nipples and then slowly outlining them with a black eyebrow pencil, while she did her eye make-up in the mirror behind me. It was a tedious, distracting task but my endless childhood labors instilled in me the proper work ethic for the job.

After the first few titillating nights of nipple-painting, I was surprised how routine and non-sexual it became in the course of the backstage hustle and bustle of the play. I did, however, make sure I never got "fired" from my new job by ensuring that she never missed an entrance and "Queen Ariadne" and I *did* end up dating for a few months.

I heard my father's voice. "Are you willing to marry this girl?" At that moment, faced with the prospect of painting her nipples every night for the run of the show, I told myself, "Yes."

The problem with deciding to be an actor but not knowing how to express your feelings, is that emotion is the currency an actor spends when he works. If you don't know how to spend your currency, you can't buy much.

Theatre is also built on conflict. If you have been taught your whole life to avoid conflict, it is very hard to feel entitled to fight for what your character wants in a scene.

The first professional acting class I took was at the Wisdom Bridge Theater on Howard Street in Chicago. It was taught by Edward Kaye-Martin, a brilliant, tempestuous man who had studied at the feet of Sanford Meisner in New York.

The Meisner Method acting technique encourages the actor to use his own experience to fill out the character's inner life, substituting powerful, personal feelings from the actor's own past to give the playwright's conflicts and characters a real sense of import and urgency. The specific, personal nature of your own experience surprisingly creates art that is universal.

Having spent my whole life on a farm in the Bible Belt in a family where it was expected that you didn't cry unless your arm was severed, and in which extreme joy is expressed in ecstatic phrases like "That's nice," I found myself at a distinct disadvantage in auditions and acting classes.

In my past experience onstage, I had pretended to have the feelings of my character, and "indicated" the necessary behavior to fool the audience into thinking it was real. It is a safe way to perform in a play, and it is fine for high school plays and community theatre, but is not very satisfying for the audience or the actor. I think that most audiences can feel the difference between someone who is faking it and someone who has worked to make their performance real.

For me, even faking emotion was fun, and occasionally I would get caught up in my own performance and I would find myself crying real tears or adrenalized with real anger. The problem was that I didn't know how to be consistent. In the professional theatre, there are eight performances a week, and I wanted to have a real experience every time I was onstage.

I understood intellectually that my character should be upset in a given scene, and I could indicate that I was upset by screwing up my face and tensing my vocal chords and pretending to wipe away tears, but I was faking it, and everyone in class knew it.

Many were the times that Ed would stop the scene I had worked so hard on with my partner and ask me what I was doing. I would start to explain it rationally.

"Well, I think my character, Tom, would be really angry in this scene--"

"You *are* Tom."

"What?"

"You *are* Tom, aren't you?"

"Well, I'm playing him in this scene."

"Then you *are* him, aren't you?"

"I guess so…"

"You can't 'guess.' You either are or you aren't." He would hold my gaze calmly, a small grin spreading across his face. The rest of the class would watch from the dark seats around him, silently relieved that it was me in his sights and not them.

"Yes, I *am* Tom."

"Good. Go on."

"Go on with the *scene*, or…?"

"Talk to me. What are you doing?"

"Well, Tom is angry because—

"Say 'I.'"

"I'm sorry?"

"Say 'I.' You *are* Tom, right? '*I* am angry because…'"

"Oh, right. *I* am angry because…"

Ed was a marvel to watch in class, particularly if you were not the one he was in the process of dissecting. He was so passionate about his belief in the transformative power of "real" acting for both the audience and the actor that he would strut passionately on the lip of the stage and pound his chest for emphasis.

Ed was confrontational and painfully honest in class, and although his critiques sometimes hurt, it was a comfort to always know exactly where you stood with him. There was no guessing how he felt. If he felt it, he said it. I had never known anyone like him. I didn't even know you were *allowed* to be like that.

Ed would try desperately to get me to express a genuine emotion in class, but I was too steeped in my Midwestern stoicism to let it out. He began to call me "Frankenstein" and would imitate the monster, walking stiffly with his arms held straight out in front of him.

He pointedly told me I would never be an actor, that I should try a modeling career instead. Despite the volcano of anger and humiliation growing inside me, all I could do was nod and internalize the anger and silently agree with him.

I *knew* he wanted me to get angry, and I could *feel* the embarrassment and rage and frustration inside me, but I had been taught my whole life to hold those feelings inside. I couldn't figure out how to let them out now.

One Tuesday, after a particularly frustrating class, I grabbed my bag and stormed out of the acting studio onto Howard Street in the middle of a sunny afternoon. I could barely see through my rage and the sudden bright sunlight, and I nearly ran into an older woman who was carrying a couple of shopping bags. I stomped toward the elevated train station and suddenly—almost as if my body were being controlled by a mysterious force—I swung around like an Olympic discus thrower, screamed and hurled my bag as hard as I could into the air.

With my own scream still ringing in my ears, I watched my bag soar through the still, blue sky, opening in mid-flight and jettisoning a stack of my recently-printed acting headshots like spent booster rockets. They fluttered like tiny parachutes to the far corners of the trash-strewn lot beside the acting school.

I sat in my disgust on the hot sidewalk with my head in my hands, further humiliated by the fact that none of the dozens of Howard Street shoppers seemed to have even noticed my cathartic eruption.

As a teenager, it had always been easier for me to purge my anger when I was alone. I had bloodied my knuckles on dozens of inanimate punching bags (appropriately, "Stop" signs were always a favorite), and the throbbing in my knuckles after a boxing match with a stop sign or a tree trunk somehow eased my sense of frustration.

Now, I was trying to change that. I'd left home and picked a career that I was perhaps not naturally suited to, just so I could learn to express this tangled mess of feelings I had been collecting and storing since I was a child. I couldn't give up now. Even my father had suggested I give it a full five years. "If at first you don't succeed, try, try again," his voice throbbed in my head.

After a moment, I got up and slowly wandered into the empty lot to retrieve my bag and my headshots, which were strewn about with the other garbage, each with my frozen face smiling blankly at the Chicago sky.

Our farmhouse, a few months after Dad bought it.
The outhouse can be seen at the bottom right.

My newlywed mother demonstrates the swing that would one day have an impact on me.

Me, in my best "baseball card" pose, with Dad's mitt, in front of our suburban home, 1966. My life was about to change drastically . . .

The Beautiful Lansing Farm.

The Brown family at "The Country", 1966
(left to right, Mom, Ferris, me, Barb and Dad).

A photo of young 'John Kinsella' for
the opening montage of *Field of Dreams.*

Photo by Melinda Sue Gordon

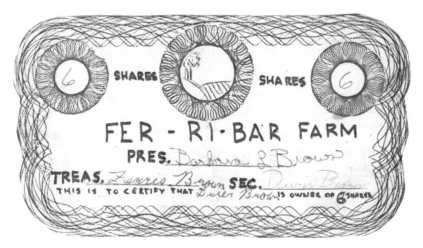

A stock certificate for Fer-Ri-Bar Farm.

Dad with his son on his shoulder,
my sister Barb in front.

'John Kinsella' with his "son"
for the opening montage of
Field of Dreams.

Dad and Mom in the creek at 'The Country' with my cousins, 1955.

'John Kinsella' proudly holds his new invention: corn.

Photo by Melinda Sue Gordon

Me, at far right, as Luther Billis, doing the "Honeybun" dance in the Highland High School production of *South Pacific*.

Da Boyz, being English fops: Steve Eastin, Art Lafleur and Charles Hoyes. Not pictured, Michael Mahurin.

Photo by Melinda Sue Gordon

My grandaddy, Fred E. Ferris, in his WWI uniform.

'John' in his WWI uniform for the opening montage, *Field of Dreams.*

Grandaddy with the Toronto Tigers, 1913. He is the tallest player, in the middle of the back row.

Photo by Melinda Sue Gordon

My father in his WWII uniform.

'John' in his WWI uniform for the
opening montage, *Field of Dreams.*

My six year-old father wins the Prince of Wales look-alike contest
on the Asbury Park boardwalk in 1927.

Hanging out on the Art Dept. truck
(left to right, Monica Baber (John Kinsella's wife), Ray Liotta
and Phil Robinson's assistant Jane DeVries).
Note the Hudson sprayer behind Ray, used to paint the dead grass green.

The Brown family at my graduation, 1976 (left to right, Dad, Mom , me,
Ferris, Barb and Grandaddy).

The ghost players on the field of dreams.

Jimmy Stewart and me.

Photo by Jane Ayer

The card I made for Dad's memorial service.

The Truth Shall Set You Free

"SHOELESS JOE: (mid 30's-early 40's) Silent, tough man with a great dignity and hidden demons. He doesn't need to say a word to exude charisma. He has the wisdom of the years in his eyes and has a large, strong, magical presence. Must be able to play baseball, to field and swing a bat with grace. Unknowns will be considered."

- Casting breakdown

Ray Liotta is a little scary. Part of it is the types of roles he plays that you can't help but project on to him. But he plays that type of role for a reason. Phil Robinson has said that when he was looking for an actor to play Shoeless Joe, he wanted someone who "could command attention without doing anything." Ray Liotta does that.

Ray was one of the first actors I met on the set because he was having his picture taken for a Shoeless Joe baseball card while I was having mine taken for Ray's opening voiceover. I ran into him at the hotel bar that night. I was wearing a comfortable old Hawaiian shirt that I had found used and threadbare at a thrift store years earlier. It was so worn-out, you could see my shoulders through the shredded fabric.

Ray was easy to spot in the bar because his intense eyes make him look like a dangerous fugitive no matter where he is. I sat down next to him.

"How did it go today?" I asked.

"Ah, it was okay I think." I had been hoping for a little more detail about the dynamic on the set.

"How is James Earl Jones?"

"He's cool. Very nice guy."

"Really?"

Ray looked at me with his serial killer eyes. "Very intimidating, though. Scary."

When my brow furrowed in confusion, he burst out with an unexpected cackle of a laugh that amplified as it bounced off the walls of the nearly deserted bar. "I'm kiddin' you." I smiled. "Relax. Have a beer." He pointed to the pitcher on the table.

I poured a glass. "So, it went well today?"

"Yeah. It's hard to tell. Phil is very quiet these days."

"What do you mean? What's he doing?"

"When I first got here, he was all talkative and fun. Now he seems depressed... What the hell happened to your shirt?" He pointed to the threadbare shoulders.

"Nothing. It's my lucky Hawaiian shirt. It's a little beat up." Before I could react, he reached up and stuck his finger through the loose threads on the shoulder of my shirt, hooked them, and pulled his finger toward him. I heard the fabric tear as he plucked his finger out of it.

"There. Now it's even luckier." He cackled again as my eyes went wide with shock.

"What are you doing?" I backed away from him.

He was still laughing. "I just made it luckier." I looked down at the small tear in the already-shredded shirt.

"This is my favorite shirt." I looked at him sharply.

His laughter died slowly as he looked at me. "Come on, it's falling apart." I stared at him, trying to look like a serial killer myself.

"It's still my shirt." He tilted his head with that *are-you-kiddin'-me?* look.

"Hey, I'm sorry. I was just kidding around." He smiled like he didn't mean it.

"Don't mess with my lucky shirt, okay?"

He smirked back.

I ended up hanging out with Ray more than any other actor on the film and he really is a funny guy. But anytime I wore my thrift-store Hawaiian shirt, he would try to hook it with his finger. He just couldn't help himself.

After a few short months away from home, living the actor's life in Chicago, I had learned how to say "I love you" and taught my family how to hug each other. Hugging was easy compared with trying to get my body to express the anger I had been storing up. My father had taught me by example to keep my anger inside because it was a burden to the people around me. My anger could hurt other people.

It became a self-fulfilling prophecy. It felt like I had a geyser building up pressure inside me. If I finally allowed a small hole to let it out, there was so much pent-up pressure that the first burst of real expression was explosively out of proportion. It then reinforced my fears that those feelings were dangerous and I would shut myself down again.

In the coming weeks, I had more and more breakthroughs in acting class, where some of the toxic anger I had been storing would erupt in a scene or improvisation. It would happen unexpectedly, when I became so focused on my character's objective that I was no longer censuring my behavior.

These outbursts scared me at first, and certainly surprised Ed and my scene partners ("Frankenstein is alive! He's alive!"). But, after it was over, the class would applaud and Ed would make sure I was okay and assure me that these powerful emotions were my "talent" and that I could learn to use them to my advantage on stage.

He helped me to understand that these feelings that I had been taught to keep inside because they weren't appropriate in my parent's house were appropriate on stage. The theatre was a safe place to have all of the emotions I wasn't allowed to have anywhere else. Applause is the audience's way of saying "thank you" for helping them to feel something that might be impossible or inappropriate in their own lives.

As Ed constantly reminded us, "Acting isn't lying; acting is telling the truth." I cannot overestimate the power of this revelation for me. Although Ed had been repeating this mantra to me *ad nauseum* in class, the day it finally reached from my ears to my heart, it was like I had been struck by a bolt of lightning. When I walked out of the doors of the dark acting classroom into the bright daylight of Howard Street, I was seeing the world as an entirely different place.

It had been scrubbed clean of all the pretense and illusion that had frustrated me my whole life. Behind every apparent lie, there was a Truth, and I knew now, finally, I had the power to see It. I felt like I was really alive for the first time. Every person waiting distractedly on the Howard Street train platform that day had a story, had a "truth" under their bored exterior and I wanted to know what it was.

This revelation made sense of the world for me for the first time. I was fired up about my career and the power that real acting could bring to people to see their own life situations clearly and to change them if necessary.

Looking at acting almost as a service to humanity was right up my Midwestern Protestant alley. It took the ego right out of it. Not only would I be able to express these forbidden emotions I had been saving up but I would also be helping people by allowing them to purge their own pent-up feelings.

In my first few months in Chicago, my whole philosophy of acting had changed. I would no longer try to fool people into believing I was someone else, I would work to become that character and reveal the truth of their situation.

I threw myself into my new mission. I became fascinated with people and watching their behavior. I imagined their secret lives and the truths they were hiding. I spent Saturday afternoons in acting class and the rest of the week thinking about what the next class would bring and rehearsing with my scene partner. I came to a new understanding of the old phrase: "The truth shall set you free." I couldn't wait to use my newly discovered super powers to change the world.

JAMES EARL

"Eventually you come to realize that most people aren't looking for a fight but for someone to surrender to."

- Robert Brault

With all of the opening voiceover shots done for *Field of Dreams*, I was sent to the hair and make-up trailer to have my old-age makeup removed and to wash the gray out of my hair. As I walked across the gravel parking lot to the trailer nestled out of camera-shot behind the slope next to the barn, I took a deep breath.

I realized how much I missed the smell of the fertile soil and a lazy creek. It seemed like I could feel the corn stalks unrolling their leaves as they twisted towards the sun. *I am shooting a movie in a cornfield,* I thought to myself proudly, as if such an absurd accomplishment had been on my list of things to do before I died.

Although I had been on the set for a couple of days, I had only met a handful of the cast and crew. Because we had been working on the still shots for the opening monologue, we were like a shadow film, on the same location, but separate from the main shooting set.

I was slowly being introduced around to be fitted and sized up and transplanted as the "real" face of John Kinsella into everyone's imaginary vision of what Ray's father might look like when they read the script. Accompanying the inevitable small talk of meeting the new face on the set, I could feel wheels turning and heads nodding thoughtfully as each person adjusted their vision to fit me in.

I suspected that everyone who had read the script had subconsciously cast their own father in the role of John Kinsella, and they were now working to imbue me with their fathers' personality traits in order to keep their own vision of the movie intact. It felt good to be looked at as the best of everyone's father.

Of all the actors who had been cast in the film, I was the most nervous to meet James Earl Jones. His voice and demeanor are so powerful and I had always been a fan of his acting in films. Because I started out as a stage actor, it had always been a dream of mine to watch one of his legendary stage performances, maybe in *Fences* or *Othello*. I knew I would be meeting him sooner or later on the set, and I wanted to be ready.

It is always awkward to talk for the first time to someone you admire. You want desperately to let them know what their particular contribution has meant to you, and sometimes that is difficult enough to express with words. You also want them to really "feel" the depth of your admiration, just as profoundly as you feel it, which is probably impossible. And then, on top of all that of course, you want to be their new best friend, to share all of their dark secrets and funny stories and have dinner together a few times a week.

As I walked the final, sunny steps to the make-up trailer, I practiced my casual introduction:

"Nice to meet you, Mr. Earl Jones" *Is it "Earl-Jones" or just "Jones"?*

"It's a pleasure to finally meet you, Mr. Jones." *"Finally?!" Who am I, Henry Morton Stanley with the ole, "Dr. Livingstone, I presume?"*

"James, I look forward to working with you." *I can't call Darth Vader "James!"*

When I arrived at the door of the make-up trailer, I knocked and yelled, "Stepping up!" I opened the door and began to climb the stairs. This is a make-up trailer courtesy, intended to warn the make-up artist that the trailer may bounce a bit as a new person steps up into it. The knock could avoid ruining an artist's perfect make-up job with a rocking trailer or, worse yet, prevent an eye-liner or a sharp brush from ending up in an actor's eye. I was proud that I had learned these little bits of set protocol during my years in Hollywood, so I wouldn't have to embarrass myself with an awkward *faux pas.*

I had also learned from my other film work that many stars are a little embarrassed by their celebrity. They didn't ask for all the attention, and although their fame allows them to continue to do the work they love, it makes them uncomfortable if you call attention to it by fawning over them or treating them as if they are some kind of royalty.

Once I was inside, I almost bumped into Bonita, one of the makeup girls, who was cleaning her brushes. She teased me about my gray hair and wrinkles and I joked that the heat and the fast-paced life in Dyersville, Iowa had aged me prematurely.

She laughed and pointed me to the chair at the far end of the small trailer by the sink and told me she would be down to remove my makeup in a minute.

It was a typical hair and make-up trailer. The wall down the left side of the trailer was marked with six identical large mirrors, each surrounded by a dozen bright, frosted globes of light. The linoleum counter that ran the length of the trailer was punctuated by small collections of beauty products, creams, powders, pencils, sprays and make-up palettes, each organized a little differently in front of its respective salon chair.

Each mirror was decorated with silly photos of the make-up artist clowning around mixed with continuity Polaroids of different actors' make-up, to be used to ensure the look was the same day-to-day, since some scenes take several days to shoot.

So distracted was I by looking at these photos, that it took me several moments to realize that a large man was sitting in the third salon chair from the door. He was a handsome, African-American man with short-cropped graying hair. Oh, God. *It was James Earl Jones.*

Fortunately, he was looking down studying his script with an intensity that kept him from noticing that I lurched visibly when I saw him, like I had walked into a coat rack in the dark. I steadied myself and moved mechanically toward my seat at the end of the room, trying to pretend that I couldn't see the entire, brilliantly-lit trailer in the wall-to-wall mirrors.

I eased casually into my salon chair and looked straight ahead at my wrinkled, old face in the mirror. This was not how I had planned to meet one of the great actors of the American stage. Unable to hold my own wizened gaze for the moment, I glanced down to the floor, frantically resuming my inner litany of potential opening lines to begin my lifelong friendship with Mr. Jones:

"What an honor to meet you, Mr. Jones" *Too grandiose.*
"What's your favorite color? (short pause) Mine, too!" *Too weird.*
"How do you make your voice—"

Suddenly, a large, smiling face was leaning toward me, hand outstretched across the empty salon chair between us. "Hi, I'm Jimmy," he said simply, in a voice that vibrated the floor of the tiny trailer and rattled the make-up pencils on the countertop. As many times as I had heard his voice onscreen, I was still not prepared to hear it in person. It rumbled through every pore of my body like an earthquake. It was a phenomenon.

I grabbed his large hand desperately, like it was a lifeline from a rescue ship. "Hi, I'm Dwier," I squeaked.

"So, you must play the father," he boomed softly, sizing me up through his wire-rimmed glasses. "Nice role." I felt his words through my chair.

I was dumbstruck by his kind eyes and welcoming smile, in contrast to the voice that seemed to emanate from the center of the Earth. "I don't always look so old," I joked about my make-up.

"Neither do I," he chuckled, looking at his reflection in the mirror, "and I don't even have on any make-up." His twinkling eyes met mine in the wall-to-wall mirrors. "But it happens." He paused, reflecting. "It's good for you. Lets you see into your future."

As the last vibrations of his voice died in the corners of the trailer, Bonita arrived and swung my chair around to remove my makeup wrinkles. As she spun me, I caught a glimpse of my father's face in the mirror. I was comforted in that moment to think that my father's face would always be there inside mine. From a certain angle, and if the light is just right, I will always be able to see him.

"I didn't even want to see your movie. I'm not even *into* baseball."

He was handsome with bright blue eyes, a California cowboy in his mid-sixties. He had taken the seat next to me in the tire store waiting room once he recognized my face. "I love horses and I'd just been ridin' with my buddy Fred and our wives and he said, 'Let's go see this baseball movie."

"Well, I went and I was enjoying the movie more than I expected to and then ole' Shoeless Joe pointed you out to Costner and before you even pulled your catcher's mask off, I knew you must be his father. It hit me like a freight train. I swear I was crying before I could even see your face. We were all cryin', but I was convulsing. I couldn't help it. I was in my cowboy gear, in my boots, they had to hold me down. Fred and my wife, they were scared for me." He was leaning in to me, his blue eyes locked on mine to make sure I was getting his point.

"Why do you think it hit you so hard?" The muffled sound of the pneumatic lug wrenches purred in the background.

"I *know* why. See, my dad was a pilot. Left for the Korean War when I was three years old. My last memory is him holding my hand at the officer's club in Victorville before he shipped out. My mom told him he had to hold my hand so I wouldn't run off into the desert and get bit by a rattlesnake. So he did. But that's all I remember. I can't even remember his voice..." He swallowed hard and continued.

"On January 1st, 1954, the Air Force declared that he was missing in action. My mom was devastated, of course, but at least there was still hope. At least he wasn't killed for sure. Every year, they assured us he'd be home for Christmas and when it didn't happen, they'd say, 'Maybe not *this* Christmas, but next Christmas.' And that's what I heard every year from the time I was five until I was…well, until I was too old to believe them anymore. All I wanted was my daddy back." His smoker's voice caught in his throat.

"Anyway, twenty years went by and my father was still "missing." I decided to file a request through the Freedom of Information Act to find out what happened to my dad. It turned out that the reports they sent me said a completely different thing than what they've been telling my mom and me.

"To make a long story short, in 1978, I went on a local talk show and I told a story about what happened to my dad based on my research and flight reports. It was a total fabrication, but I'm Irish and I was a little pissed and I just didn't care anymore. The station ran my phone number and by the time I got home, there were a dozen calls on my answering machine from other people who had missing fathers and husbands.

"I couldn't believe it—I had thought I was alone.

"So, when I was watching *Field of Dreams* that day, I completely fell apart because, for me, it was the perfect expression of the longing I had been feeling inside for my father. I mean, I never even got a chance with him. I was only three years old…" He ran his hand through his salt-and-pepper hair.

"That movie gave all of us MIA families a way to explain how we'd been feeling. It gave us a rallying point to build an organization to help get closure and compensation. In a CNN interview, the guy asks me, 'What do you want?' I said, 'I'd give ten years of my life to spend a day with my dad.'"

He looked at me and paused as the impossibility of that dream washed over him.

"It's crazy that I'm talking to you now because just six months ago on Memorial Day 2013, they finally had a ceremony at Arlington National Cemetery. Almost sixty years later, they finally put up a marker for my dad and his crew."

"That must have felt good."

"It was an unbelievable relief to me. To finally put my father to rest…"

An unintelligible name is called over the staticky waiting room speakers. My new friend looks up and then touches my arm with his hand.

"And get this—this is weird that I happened to run into you today. Just three days ago, I had a dream about my father. First dream I've ever had about him."

"We're at an airfield and my dad is walking toward me and he's laughing and smiling." He looked like he was imagining it all again as he told me the story. "There are two planes behind him, sitting on the runway; a P-51 Mustang and A-36 training plane. Dad says to me, 'Let's go fly together. Which plane do you want?'

"I said, 'I don't know how to fly so I'll take the training plane; you take the Mustang.' So we take off and, next thing you know, we're flying by each other…" The tough cowboy started re-enacting the planes buzzing by each other, waving his hands around in big, curvy figure-eights like a ten year-old boy.

"And, in the dream, I can see my dad's face smiling and laughing and he's waving at me as we fly by each other, and I'm waving back at him and it's just the most amazing experience." His face held onto the dream a moment longer as his eyes brimmed with tears. "And then I woke up."

His intense blue eyes found mine again but they are softer now. He exhales. "Then three days later, I run into you, the father from *Field of Dreams*. Can you believe it?"

A Trip To The Country

"I'll guide the conversations, like taking a car around a long, gentle curve in the road,
and we'll hardly realize that we're talking of love, and family, and life,
and beauty, and friendship and sharing."

-W.P. Kinsella, *Shoeless Joe*

In 1986, at the end of a long summer in L.A., I took a trip back to Ohio for my 10-year Highland High School reunion. My high school class (the Spirit of '76) had always been close and a few of my classmates had even come out to visit me in my various apartments in Hollywood and Venice Beach.

Recently, my friend Mark Kuhar, who had been a creative writing major at Ohio University, had sent me a new book to read that he thought was really special, *Shoeless Joe* by W.P. Kinsella. I loved it, too. I looked forward to seeing him at the reunion and talking to him about it.

I was "between gigs," the euphemism for unemployed among my actor friends. For some reason, I had begun to be curious about my parents again. Maybe it was their age; maybe it was mine. I had spent my young adulthood fighting my Oedipal battles and rejecting my parents' values and proving just how different and cool and independent I really was. Now I wanted to come home to Mom and Dad.

On the plane home it occurred to me that I didn't really know much about my parents. For instance, it had only recently occurred to me that, once upon a time, they had probably been two separate people. They had been together so long (32 years) and done such an effective job of presenting a unified front, that I had lost track of their individuality.

I was so accustomed to them being there that I almost failed to see them at all. My father was a man whose blood ran through my veins, whom I had lived with for almost twenty years, and who had taught me much of what I knew about being a man *and*, because of his secrecy about his family, I was in the dark about what made him tick.

I mean, I knew the basics.

My father was born Walter Warren Brown on March 7, 1921, the third son of a well-to-do banker and businessman and his homemaker wife. His oldest brother, four years his senior, Edward Irving Brown IV, was named for his father and went on to become a wealthy businessman, worth over 40 million dollars. Next was my Uncle Bill, then my father, and two years later, they gave him a little sister, Barbara.

I had seen pictures of my father as a small boy with a blond Dutch-boy haircut, sitting on a pony, holding a polo mallet, as he won the Prince of Wales Look-alike contest at the nearby boardwalk. Other than that, he had told me very little about the rest of his childhood.

He survived the worst hard times of his generation, the Depression and WWII, where he was a tail-gunner instructor for the Army Air Corps. His college education was interrupted by the war, but he returned to college on the G.I. bill, and, at the age of 28, he earned a degree in Architecture from the University of Illinois in Champaign. He met my mother at a young adult church group while he was visiting his brother Bill in Pittsburgh.

My father was a quiet man at a time when assertive men changed the world. He liked to make children laugh, by pretending to pull coins from their ears or tickling them, in a little game he called "johnnywalker." He was never more light-hearted than when he was recalling how they had "razzed" so-and-so at work. He had a corny sense of humor that was both endearing and embarrassing to me.

With other men, he always seemed a bit awkward, a bit wide-eyed, a bit wary, always careful not to offend.

Even when talking with men who were asking permission to hunt rabbits and pheasants on our farm, where my father clearly held the power position, his face betrayed a look of apology and deference. It is an expression I never understood, but one I feel on my own face more often than I'd like.

After a few days of catching up with my high school friends, I over-heard my dad talking about having to drive down to The Country to close up the tiny summer cottage where my mother had spent summers as a child and where our family had spent a week of our summer vacation every year.

My mother never really liked the place (I suppose it reminded her of long summers isolated with her mother and her cold, stern father), but my dad loved it. When I was seven, he had taken it on himself to install running water and indoor toilets and, of course, to dig a basement. When my mother decided she couldn't go with him because of her promise to help at a church function, I said, "I'll go."

"Really?" said my dad, surprised.

"Yeah, why not?" I said. " Sounds like fun. I haven't been to The Country in, what, ten years?" Our family's nickname for my late Grand-daddy's house was a little ironic. True, the property was remote, but our own 52-acre farm in northeastern Ohio wasn't exactly urban.

"Are you sure?" asked my dad, "We'll have some work to do."

"Let's do it," I replied, sounding more excited than I was. It wasn't that I didn't want to go, but I suddenly wasn't sure what I was getting myself into. I hadn't spent four hours alone with my father...well, in my whole life. With my oldest sister only two years older than I, and a brother in between, most family events involved all of us. Two hours each way, in a car, with nowhere to hide... I could see from my father's expression that he wasn't so sure about it either.

So it was with some trepidation that I climbed behind the wheel of my parent's small, sensible Chevy Chevette, and with my father riding shotgun, we said goodbye to Mom and headed southeast.

My Dad loved "shortcuts." If he could take six zig-zag country roads to save 200 yards of straight interstate highway, that was the way we went. Ours was the perfect destination for his navigation style—there were no straight roads to the middle of this nowhere.

I was aware, while talking myself into this trip, that the reason I knew so little about my father was that he had never told us much. We had taken the meandering tour of his seemingly countless childhood homes in the Asbury Park area of central New Jersey. We had spent two-week vacations with my grandmother at the last of her homes in Belmar, a plain, 3-story Victorian house on a quiet street six blocks from the beach. But there had always been a vague fog around his childhood and he had never told us much about his father, who died when I was just a toddler.

"How are things going out West?" he asked, interrupting my line of thought.

"Pretty well, Dad."

"Are you making a living?"

"I'm getting by. I'm taking a class that should help me get more work."

"Why are you waiting for someone else to give you a job? Why don't you just write yourself a movie and make it yourself. Like you did when you were a kid."

"That's… just not how it works out there, Dad. It's hard to get anybody to look at your stuff unless you're already famous. *Then*, you can start to make your own movies."

My reticence was waning as we swerved down the two-lane roads I vaguely remembered as a child, through towns with familiar names like Minerva and Carrollton and our childhood favorite, Paris, Ohio, which was little more than a crossroads with an abandoned gas station (we loved to tell our friends we had been to Paris on our summer vacation). I was happy to have Dad navigating and just telling me where to turn, so I could concentrate on looking for remembered landmarks and simultaneously distract him from being suspicious about my questions concerning his past and our secret family history.

At my prompting, my father told me about his first jobs stocking shelves at the A & P Market and selling ice cream with his best friend, our "Uncle" Doug, who later became an Army chaplain. He smiled when he talked about their sharing a small room in a Baltimore home before WWII, while working opposite shifts at the Glenn L. Martin airplane factory, so "the bed never got cold because one of us was always sleeping in it while the other was working."

Some of these stories I had heard before, in snippets at family events, but it was nice to hear them again in more detail. I enjoyed seeing my father smiling when I glanced at him. I kept directing the conversation as I drove the car slowly through the countryside, the roads getting ever windier as we moved into the hilly country that surrounds the Ohio River valley.

When I asked how it happened that his eldest brother Ed, whom we had always called Uncle Buster, had become a wealthy airport-owning businessman, he hesitated a moment before he began to tell the story.

"Buster was old enough that he chose to stay with your Grandfather

Brown, my father. And your grandpa was pretty well off. This was during the Depression. He owned a hotel and a bank and a few other businesses. Buster was smart enough to go with him. Bill and Barb and I stayed with Mom. I don't know how much help Dad gave him with money, but *do* I know *we* didn't have any."

"What do you mean, 'smart enough to go with him?'" Another long pause as he looked absently at the map.

"When I was about eight years old, my father met a woman named Ann. He left us to move in with her in an apartment across town. He asked my mother for a divorce, but she refused to give it to him for religious reasons, which never made much sense to me, but I was just a kid."

Now my father's voice got quieter and he looked blankly at the map in his hands. As his breathing got shallower, I watched him from the corner of my eyes and started driving slower. His shoulders dropped forward.

"My father stopped giving us money for food, so we had nothing to eat. He was trying to blackmail my mother into giving him a divorce by cutting us off. He was a rich man, my father—like I said, he owned a big hotel and a bank." Dad turned to me with a pleading look in his eyes. I nodded numbly and then pretended to concentrate on the road.

"I remember having to walk over to his office at the bank to beg him for a nickel for bread." His hands gripped the map and he swallowed hard. "He would make me wait out in the lobby all day, in front of everyone." His voice was getting softer. I leaned toward him to hear. "Finally he came out of his office and looked down at me, sitting on the floor of his bank..." He paused. Out of the corner of my eye, I saw my eight year-old father sitting next to me. "I can still see him standing over me, looking down."

My father's breath became halting and his eyes began to water. He stared blankly at the fogged-up windshield. All the air had left the car. We were passing a truck turnout and I pulled the car off the road. I felt sick and responsible.

I had never seen my father cry.

Now I wanted to go back. Back to the straight roads of the interstate; back to the safety of our silent home; back to the secrets he had never wanted me to know, to the pain he hadn't wanted to remember.

I reached my hand across his shoulder but the bucket seats kept us apart. "I'm sorry, Dad..." I offered lamely. His strong body shook under my hand and he finally turned to me abruptly, almost accusingly.

"I didn't blame him for having an affair! I had friends whose fathers had left them, but they always took care of their kids. Why didn't he take care of us?" he pleaded. I wanted to answer him. I wanted to make it all right, to fix it, to make it all go away. Then my 65 year-old father turned and crumpled onto the dashboard, crying the lost tears of an eight year-old boy.

My hand stroked the soft cotton of his flannel shirt. I was panicked. *Now I've done it, I thought. I've broken through his tough exterior, now what?* I'd always wanted to know what was behind my father's stoic façade and now I just wanted him to stop crying. Helplessly, I reached for the car's defroster to clear the fogged-up windshield.

It all made sense now. My father's secrets and his sense of duty, his insistence on family loyalty and his almost exhaustive need to spend time with us when we were little—even when it felt like he was doing it for some hidden reason. Like he was looking up at his dad, saying "I'll show you! THIS is how to take care of your children!"

My father kept crying despite his efforts to stop. Just as he would calm down, another wave would come and his body would rack with sobs. I leaned across the gearshift and draped myself on his rounded back. His body was still heaving. In that moment I wanted to take back every unkind word I'd ever said, every unloving thought I'd ever had, every lie I had ever told him. I laid my head on his back and watched the fan clear diagonal lines across the bottom of the windshield.

"I'm sorry, Dad." With my ear on his warm back, I could hear his halting breath slowly come back to him. I stroked his shoulder for a long time. "I didn't know any of that stuff."

He slowly sat up to pull his handkerchief out of his pocket and he blew his nose loudly. I leaned back into my seat and cranked open my window. The storm had passed but I could tell he had been embarrassed by it. "I didn't see any reason to tell you."

"Well, I'm glad you did." I wanted him to look at me so he would know it was alright. He didn't.

"It's water under the bridge. Nothing I can do about it now." Of course he was right.

"I don't know, Dad. Sometimes it helps just to talk about things. Let them out."

"Does it?"

"*I* think so. I'm glad to know a little bit more about you—that's a good thing, isn't it?" He said nothing. His brow furrowed again. His eyes were red, his face puffy. His perfect white hair was tousled.

"I love you, Dad."

There was a pause as the four small words hung in the heavy air, trapped in the tiny car with us.

"Thank you," he said, so softly I almost didn't hear him.

LIKE BEING DIPPED IN
MAGIC WATERS

"A man knows he is growing old because he begins to look like his father."
- Gabriel Garcia Marquez

T he sudden exposure of his secret pain changed something between my father and me. Seeing his vulnerability for the first time in my life, I felt stronger and more capable. I didn't feel superior to him, as if I'd found his weakness; on the contrary, exposing his childhood pain to me made me feel deferential and protective towards him.

The windshield had finally cleared by the time we reached Grandaddy's cottage. I drove down the long, overgrown driveway, and slowed to a crawl across the rumbly wooden bridge over the creek, the way my father had always done to surprise my grandparents with our arrival. I brought the car to a stop under the carport my father had built for his in-laws.

Dad climbed out of the car slowly, easing the stiffness out of his knee and we both inhaled the sweet, dense country air. The smell of pine, walnut, sycamore and sassafras crowded our senses the same way they crowded the long, narrow driveway, as if the aromas had saved themselves all summer, waiting for us to inhale them.

To relieve the tension of my father's tearful confession, we started right to work. Dad unlocked the door and the smell of the cold kerosene heater filled the small, dark cottage. Hundreds of National Geographic magazines on shelves lined the walls of the cluttered dining room. Dad looked around while I brought the storm shutters up from the basement.

We drained the water pipes to prevent them from freezing. I hurried to lift the plywood storm panels my father had built to cover the screened-in porch so Dad would have the easier job of closing the hook-and-eyes on either side to hold them in place. He had done the same for my brother and me when we were too little to lift them as kids.

The whole cottage was smaller than I remembered and closing it up was like shutting up a dollhouse to carry it home. We had finished the work in a few hours and had loaded the car by late afternoon.

Before we left, I asked Dad to walk with me through the sloping field to the swimming hole we had spent so many summer days damming up and swimming in. The creek, too, was smaller than I remembered but the water looked so clear and inviting that I suggested we "take a dip", using my father's favorite expression to entice him.

"I didn't bring my bathing suit."

"Neither did I. Who cares? We could skinny dip." The words were out of my mouth before I thought about who I was talking to. I was about to succumb to my embarrassment and laugh off the invitation, when instead, I pulled off my sweaty t-shirt.

"We don't have towels."

"We'll air dry."

I had never even *seen* my father naked and I had just invited him to skinny dip. Dad wasn't exactly enthusiastic, but he followed my lead and slowly took off his clothes and placed them carefully on a large sandstone boulder, partially enveloped by the roots of a smooth, spreading sycamore tree.

I jumped into the cold water with a scream the way my dad had taught us to and kept screaming while my head was underwater. I bobbed to the surface giggling with the thrill of the cool water on my naked skin. The slimy rocks felt good under my feet and I walk-swam to the shallow end pretending to look for crayfish while my father finished undressing and slowly waded in. He looked older and heavier and more fragile than I remembered. The sight of him walking stiffly on the mossy rocks stabbed at my heart for a moment so I couldn't breathe.

I stared down into the shallow water looking through my own reflection and the canopy of trees above me. I remembered Dad showing us how to find the crayfish in their hiding places under the rocks. Flipping the rock upstream would cause a cloud of mud to drift across the exposed area, allowing the crayfish to dart away to another hiding place, while flipping it downstream exposed them in clear water. We had filled many a mason jar with crayfish before we would dump them back in the creek and use the same jars to fill with lightning bugs at night.

When I looked up again, Dad was moving smoothly through the water, his shock of white hair reflecting wildly in the ripples. I was 27 and my dad was 65 and we were swimming naked together in Grandaddy's creek.

"Did we used to dam the creek *here?*" I asked, pointing to a narrow spot downstream. Dad looked.

"It's all so different now. I think it was closer—more like right here."

I picked up a slippery plate-sized rock from the bottom and tossed it to where he had pointed and then grabbed another. I threw a few more into a rough line across the creek and he joined me, tossing rocks into our makeshift dam, like we had done for fifteen summers in a row when I was a kid.

Soon, without thinking, we were dam-building in earnest. I wrestled a boulder from the suction of the muddy bottom and rolled it toward the dam. I remembered as a kid watching my father move impossibly large rocks out of the swimming hole onto the dam and him explaining how much lighter they are if you move them under the water, due to buoyancy and water displacement and other science I could no longer remember. Why was it always easier to talk to my dad when we were working on a project?

In twenty minutes, the water in the swimming hole was rising noticeably. Startled crayfish scurried for cover as two grown men thrashed around with slimy rocks in the muddy water, both increasingly oblivious to the fact that they were naked.

When the enthusiasm for the dam had waned, we sat on warm rocks and wrestled our clothes on over still-damp skin. I helped my father up through the wild raspberry thorns on the bank of the creek and out of the trees that line the creek bed and we headed to the car.

The thick, overgrown grass was already wicking the dew from the soft soil and the lightning bugs crawled up the long blades to start their evening flight.

I took one last deep inhale as I climbed into the car. Dad fell asleep after just a few minutes on the road and I slipped the map out of his folded hands and decided to take a shortcut home.

LOST FATHER, LEGENDARY COACH

"Dad taught me every thing I know.
Unfortunately, he didn't teach me everything he *knows."*

– Al Unser

Brian Frankish was 45 years old when he was asked by Phil Robinson to act as Executive producer and Unit Production Manager for *Shoeless Joe*. Holding those two jobs, Brian was essentially in charge of overseeing every aspect of the production and making sure the movie got made on time and on budget.

Brian was born in June of 1942 and his father Jack was drafted into the Army six months later. Jack was assigned to be a war correspondent in Belgium and became the boss of a young war reporter named Walter Cronkite. Jack Frankish was killed on Dec. 23, 1944, at the Battle of the Bulge, when Brian was only eighteen months old.

Brian built a legend around the father he didn't know, based on stories from his mother and a wartime letter his father had written for him should he be killed in battle. It was given to Brian on his sixteenth birthday.

Forty years later, Brian needed a baseball consultant for the movie to help them cast the ballplayers and coach them to play in the style of 1920's players. They decided to start looking close to home, inviting legendary former University of Southern California coach Rod Dedeaux to the Toluca Lake Golf Course to discuss helping them out.

Even at 74, Dedeaux was a busy man, full of energy, running his own successful trucking business and he was not inclined to help out a production company making a baseball film. Dedeaux was critical of "the phoniness that was in baseball movies," an opinion he acquired while working as an extra in the 1948 film *The Babe Ruth Story*.

When he arrived at the golf course restaurant where Phil and Brian were waiting, he clapped them on the shoulder as he shook their hands and greeted them with a typical "Hiya, Tiger!"

After the movie folks had given him their pitch, Dedeaux gently explained his dislike for baseball movies and his reticence to commit to the project. They tried a few other ploys to convince him, but to no avail. Finally, during a lull in the meeting, Dedeaux blurted, "Brian, are you any relation to a Jack Frankish?"

Brian was puzzled for a moment by this nonsequitir. "Yeah, he was my father. He was killed in WWII."

"Well, I was a student at USC in 1933 and your father was my best friend."

This amazing coincidence sparked a new wave of nostalgic conversation, and Frankish got to hear about his father as a young man for the first time, through the eyes of his father's best friend.

Dedeaux agreed to read the script.

A few days later, he called Frankish to tell him he'd be honored to help out the son of his best friend from college. He even convinced his former player and Baltimore Orioles standout Don Buford to give him a hand.

Rod Dedeaux had coached at USC for 45 seasons, won 28 conference championships and 11 national titles. He was named "Coach of the

Century" by *Collegiate Baseball* magazine.   He coached dozens of future major league players, including Tom Seaver, Mark McGuire, Dave Kingman and Randy Johnson.

Dedeaux accepted a salary of only $1 per year when he was coaching at USC because of his successful trucking business. He had turned down offers to coach in the major leagues with the Dodgers and others, because he loved the college game and he wanted to stay close to his family.

One day on the set, between setups, Phil asked him, "Hey, coach, what position did you play?"

"I was a shortstop," Dedeaux replied, smiling.

"Really, could you—were you good?" Phil asked. The coach became pensive.

"I could field the ball."

"Could you hit?" asked Phil.

"I could hit the ball." Dedeaux replied quietly.

"Well, how come you never played in the majors?"

Coach said, "I did."

"Really?" asked Phil, surprised.

"Yes, in 1935, I was the starting shortstop for the Brooklyn Dodgers." He paused. "I played one game, broke my back, and that was the end of my playing career."

Phil's face went white. "Oh my God, you're Doc Graham," he whispered.

"That's right," Dedeaux said. There was a quiet moment.

Phil finally asked, "Do you ever think about, 'Gee, the career I might've had?'"

"Every day," Coach said, smiling, and he walked away across the infield.

SINK OR SWIM

"This is one moment but soon another shall pierce you
with a painful joy."
-T.S.Eliot

The second I saw him, I knew he was going to die. "Hi, Dad, how are you feeling?" I stuttered, forcing myself to smile.

"Ah, not too bad."

"It's so good to see you." I paused. "I missed you."

"Thank you." He paused. "How was your flight?"

"It was fine. I slept."

"When did you get in?"

"Just an hour ago. I came right here."

"Oh. Good. It's good to see you."

"It's good to see *you*," I repeated. It reminded me of one of those awkward conversations after you've just watched a terrible show your friend is in and you don't want to lie but you can't exactly tell the truth, either, so you fumble desperately for meaningless things to talk about and desperately fumble to make them sound important.

It was the smell that brought me back to the room I was standing in. The sour smell of urine and antiseptic and food without flavor. The too white, too clean, too bright atmosphere of polite colors and the relentless linoleum, sprawling like shiny, fresh ice into every corner.

The white sheets exaggerated my father's sallow skin. He had always had olive skin, but now it was a dim yellow, like a spent glowstick.

It was his color that had first sent him to the doctor over a month before. I had already purchased airline tickets to come home a week later to see my family before I went to Iowa, when my mom called to tell me Dad was in the hospital. She hadn't wanted to worry me. Yet something had told me to change my tickets and come home right away. Now here I was looking at my father lying in a maze of tubes and wires.

My brother and sister came in with my mom and stood at the foot of my father's bed. Nobody spoke. A large, smiley nurse asked me to move from the bedside so she could check my father's I.V. I told Dad, "I'll be right back," and ushered my family into the hallway.

"So, what's going on?" I asked.

My brother had told me on the way in from the airport that the doctors were unsure what to do, but nobody had told me it was *this* bad. It was clear to me now that my father was near death. I think the rest of my family knew it, too, but nobody wanted to tell my mom because they had spent the past month "being positive" and trying to keep my dad's spirit's up by avoiding the obvious. They had been so successful at "being positive" that I had been given no idea that my father was even sick.

"Mrs. Brown?" A short, stocky doctor in a striped dress shirt and tie appeared behind me. He looked down at his chart. "Elsie?" He was dark-skinned, with a trimmed beard that went high onto his cheeks and reading glasses that were barely hanging onto the end of his nose.

My mother emerged from our huddle. "Hello, Dr. Ansari, how are you?" she said with the same polite tone she greeted people with after church.

"I'm fine, thank you."

"This is my son, Dwier, and my daughter, Barbara, who just got in this morning…"

"Nice to meet you," he said. "I've heard a lot about you."

"Thank you," my sister and I said in unison. We all laughed a little.

"…and you know my other son, Ferris," she turned toward my brother, now behind her.

"Yes, good to see you again." He looked down at his clipboard absently and inhaled slowly. "I'm afraid I don't have good news for you."

"Your husband's blood has reached a critical point. We had hoped to determine why his liver has stopped functioning, so we could attempt to reverse the contamination…" He stopped abruptly and searched the chart through his teetering glasses. "You are sure he does not drink alcohol?"

"Yes. Maybe a beer every few years or so."

"No, no, that would not be sufficient to…" He trailed off. "And he was negative for Hep C so…we are at a loss." He paused again. My mother still smiled. He forged on. "At this point there is nothing we can do to reverse the contamination of the blood. It is too late even for the dialysis to work." He paused. "I don't know what to say. I'm sorry."

"How long does he have?"

"We can give him something to take away the pain, but it may not be long at all."

My father had made it clear to my mother that he was not interested in being kept alive by machines. After we talked about our options, we decided to keep him as comfortable as possible and let nature take its course.

Even in the ten minutes I had been out of the room, my father's appearance had deteriorated considerably. Later, it occurred to me that he had been hanging on for weeks with all his strength until my sister and I arrived, so he could relax in the comfort of knowing his entire family was around him. "You'll have your family for your *whole* life," he would always say as an excuse to get us to stop bickering.

"Hey, Pop." His eyes fluttered open. It took him a moment to remember where he was, despite the incessant beeping of the stacks of monitors around him.

"Hey, Ricky." It was comforting to have him call me by my childhood nickname. "Where's your mom?"

"She's out talking with the doctors. She'll be back in a minute. How are you feeling?"

"I'm okay." He adopted a casual tone. "Hey, can I talk to you for a minute while Mom is out there?"

"Sure, Dad, what's going on?"

His puffy eyes filled with tears. "I don't mean to scare you, but I don't think I'm going to live much longer." He looked in my eyes to see if I was going to argue with him. I looked back, frozen like a deer sensing a predator. I nodded.

"I don't want to worry your mom, because she has been working so hard to be positive and I don't want to disappoint her." This was my father's family legacy right to the end—everyone keeping little secrets so as not to hurt someone else's feelings.

"We'll take care of Mom," I offered tentatively. His face relaxed and then his brow knit again. "What are you thinking about?" I asked. It was a question I had put to him a hundred times in the last ten years when his eyes would become fixed and his face would go blank as he fought something in his mind.

His attention came back to me with my question, but reluctantly, as if he wanted to protect me from his fight. "I don't know... what's... on the other side." He looked up into my eyes to make sure I was following. "No one's ever gone over and come back to tell us..."

I leaned toward him through the hanging vines of I.V. tubes and monitor wires and laid my chest on his, my elbows awkwardly resting on his tilted mattress. My face was buried in the starched sheets next to his and I inhaled his sickness. I wanted it all. The bleached sheets, his cool yellow skin, his septic smell, his teary yellow eyes and his strong arms taped with tubes now gently resting on my shoulders.

I stayed there for a long time, my hot breath rebounding off the hospital's crisp pillow, my right hand touching his soft, white hair. *Why had I never touched my father's hair before?* I had always loved his fine, white hair combed straight back, snow white since he was in his early forties, since shortly after we children were born he would always joke.

"I love you, Dad."

Into the collar of my shirt behind my right ear, I felt his breath. "I love you too, Ricky."

I stayed leaning over my father until I could feel his heart beating faintly next to mine. I would have stayed longer, but the nurse had entered the room behind me and was checking the monitors. "Let's try not to get everyone all upset now," she chided gently. *Fuck you!*, I thought but did not say as I handed my father a tissue from the Kleenex box by his bed.

Without discussing it, for the next few hours, my sister and brother and I started taking turns giving my mom a break from the bedside vigil she had been conducting alone for the last few weeks. We would huddle in hushed tones whenever there was a doctor to talk to or new information to process or visitors to greet.

It feels to me, as I recall it now, that I was alone at my father's hospital bed for long stretches of time. I don't know why that would have happened or if I was just so focused on soaking up every last second of his time with me that I simply don't remember anyone else in the room. His death was a singular experience for me. I took it personally. He was leaving *me*.

In the next three hours, as the morphine in his I.V. drip increased and his bed was moved to the intensive care unit, I listened to my father talk about the regrets of his life. I hadn't even known that he had started med school at Johns Hopkins in 1942, but had given up the idea when he joined the army. Occasionally, he would wince in pain and the nurse would adjust the drip.

He wished he had never taken the job with U.S. Gypsum that had forced him to travel when we were young. I reminded him that he left that job after only a year for that very reason.

I listened to him blame himself for all of the mistakes of his life and I recounted stories to refute them and thanked him for all the things he had done right, all the time he had spent with us at home and on summer vacations, in Boy Scouts and Indian Guides, creating Fer-Ri-Bar Farm and sending us all to college.

I held my father's cool hand and told him I loved him and that he was a great father, over and over again. I told him that he didn't need to fight anymore and to just relax. I listened to his breathing get slower and slower and slower. I kept whispering in his ear as the time between his breaths became impossibly long until, finally, the next inhale never came.

He lumbered slowly toward the tiny, hot springs dressed only in his underwear and boots, looking like a sasquatch that had been sold to the circus. He was huffing a bit from the climb up the mountain and had to pause at intervals to heave his lungs full of the cool, pine-scented air. Even from my vantage point in the steamy water, I could tell he was a big guy, maybe 6′4″ and 250, with a full beard and dark, unruly hair.

He grunted as he wrestled off his kayak-sized hiking boots and spread his sweaty t-shirt out on a giant chunk of granite in the dappled sunlight to dry. Coarse, black hair billowed from every inch of his pale skin.

I threw him a non-committal "Hey" as he navigated his body into the water and he mumbled back a "Howdy" as he settled his bulk onto a submerged boulder on the downstream side of the pool. I leaned back onto the rocks behind me, closed my eyes and relaxed into the sound of the natural hot spring water tumbling down the side of the mountain.

When I opened my eyes a few minutes later, Sasquatch was looking at me. I forced a smile. "Do I know you?" he asked suspiciously.

"I don't think so," I replied confidently. I was pretty sure I would have remembered this guy if I'd ever met him before. He kept staring at me.

"Where are you from?" Sasquatch sounded more articulate than I imagined he would be.

"I'm originally from Ohio, but I live in L.A. now. How about you?" I asked. This mountain man had already piqued my curiosity.

"I moved to Taos a year ago—" He stopped abruptly and his eyes went wide. "You're that guy," he sputtered. "Aren't you? That guy from that movie, the father, aren't you?" His eyes were a little wild and the steam from the hot pool added to the effect. "You are. Aren't you?"

"Yep, that was me." I leaned forward to shake his hand and suddenly remembered I was completely naked. I stopped in mid-lean. "My name's Dwier." He grabbed my hand with his massive paw and I settled sheepishly back onto my seat on the rock.

"Nice to meet you. I'm David." He looked at me, shaking his head, his white teeth now peering through the undergrowth of his beard. "I love that movie," he said. "Seen it probably a dozen times." He nodded, absently watching his giant hands squeeze hot water into tiny geysers on the surface of the pool. "I wouldn't be here if it weren't for that movie."

I thought for a second. "What do you mean by that?" I asked. "'Wouldn't *be* here' alive, or 'wouldn't be *here*' in this hot spring?"

He smiled to himself. "Both," he said.

"Wow," I said casually, inviting him to go on.

"My dad was a lawyer, a wonderful man. Kind, generous, smart. Everybody loved him—me included. He would help out people who needed it, with legal advice, whatever. A little like Doc Graham from the movie, only the "lawyer" version." He abruptly looked down into the steamy water, the tangled mass of black curls tumbling off the top of his head and teasing the curls of steam.

A breeze blew a faint smell of sulphur across the pool. I waited for him to finish his story. "He died of a heart attack when I was fifteen. Broke my heart."

"But I knew what I had to do. Decided right then and there. I was going to grow up and be a lawyer and be just like him, to show everybody how much I loved him. Show *him*, too. Because I had been so young and it was all so sudden, I never felt like I had a chance to tell him.

"So I went to college, pre-law. Same school my dad went to. And it was hard. Law school was damned hard. Never came easy to me. But I worked at it and I got my diploma, finally passed the bar (on my *third* try) and hung my shingle, just like my daddy.

"And I *hated* it. Couldn't *stand* it. Listening to people complain about this and that. The hypocrisy of the justice system. Hated it. Tried to listen and joke around and be calm like my daddy was, but the whole thing just made me sick. Literally. I couldn't sleep. I gained a bunch of weight. I got a skin condition and I started to lose patches of my hair. I was a mess." It was hard to imagine this guy without hair.

"Because I was hating my work so much, one day I decided to play hooky and go to the movies. I didn't care what movie it was, as long as it wasn't a courthouse movie. *Field of Dreams?* Definitely didn't sound like a lawyer movie, so I went."

"I'm watching it and watching it, and I'm not even a baseball fan, but I'm enjoying the story and Costner is great. It's one of those things where, I'm aware the movie is getting close to the end and I'm excited to find out what happens but at the same time, I don't want it to end. You know what I mean?"

I nodded.

"So, when Shoeless Joe points to you at the end, and Ray sees his father, I just fall apart. Tears are pouring down my cheeks but I can't look away. Here I am this big guy, a lawyer no less, and I'm blubbering like a baby. And I don't care. I can't barely breathe because I'm crying so hard, but I'm trying to be quiet so I can hear what he says to him.

"So the movie ends and I just sit there. My shirt and tie are a mess. I'm soaked from crying and sweating and the credits finish and there's that 'For Our Parents' at the end, and that just hits me. Hard. Right in the heart. 'For Our Parents.'

"And I realize what I've been doing for my dad. How I've been making myself miserable to try to be like him, all to show him how much I love him, and all he would want is for me to be happy. It's crazy."

"So what happened?"

"Well, it was hard, but I had to start trying to figure out what *I* wanted. It took me a while."

"So what did you do?"

"Well, I had always wanted to learn how to weld, so I took a class at night. And I loved it. I decided to stop shaving every day and I let all this grow out." He waved his paw at his head. "I stopped taking on new cases at my office. I just said 'no.' I slowly finished all the cases I had already started but, finally, there came a day when I didn't have any more cases. So I took down my sign and I stopped being a lawyer.

"Down at the community college, I had begun welding these giant pieces of metal together, but now the class was over. So, I built this big hoist in my back yard and I've been making my sculptures ever since. And it's all because of that movie. So it's just so weird to see you up here, sitting here in the springs. I mean, what're the odds?" He looked at me earnestly for a moment as if I might actually *know* the outrageous odds of our strange meeting.

"Wow. That's incredible." I said, letting his story swirl over the steaming water. Abruptly he threw his giant, furry head under the water, massaged it vigorously with his paws and emerged with wild eyes and a growl of satisfaction. Hot water fell through his coarse hair and beard and funneled itself into a single stream that trickled from his chin.

"How's it been going? Your new life?" I asked tentatively.

He thrust out his arms toward the towering pines, showing off his impressive, hairy wingspan. "I'm here, aren't I? On a Monday morning?" As he folded in his arms, he became suddenly pensive, almost embarrassed by his outburst. He continued softly.

"I'm happy. That's the main thing. Life is short—my dad taught me that. *He* was happy. And I was trying to be *him*, instead of being happy myself. I still help people out with their legal problems, just like my dad did, but they're not *my* legal problems. You know what I mean?"

I nodded, watching the steam drift across the surface of the hot pool. There was a long silence as the big man let out a sigh, his story finally told. He leaned against the boulder behind him and casually asked,

"What's Costner like?"

FINAL SCENE

"It gets late early out there."

– Yogi Berra

A s soon as someone figures out that I was in the movie *Field of Dreams*, the first thing they want to know is, "What's Costner like?"

I didn't meet Kevin Costner until two days after I arrived in Dyersville, because I had been busy shooting still photos and Kevin was busy shooting the movie. I had seen him a couple times on the set in passing, but, to be honest, I was a little intimidated by him and didn't want to make a big deal about meeting him, for two reasons.

For one thing, EVERYONE wanted to meet Kevin. And why not? He was hot off his success in *Bull Durham*, a rising star with a fantastic smile and an engaging personality. I admired him. Everything I had read about him had made me like him more.

He had struggled at the beginning of his career, working as a janitor at a small Hollywood studio to make ends meet. He had gotten a part in a major Lawrence Kasdan film (*The Big Chill*), only to be left on the cutting room floor, except for the scenes in which he is a corpse and his face isn't seen.

But he had persevered. And he was starting to take his success to the next level by forming his own production company and creating and writing projects for himself. The offices for his Tig Productions were at Raleigh Studios, the same tiny Hollywood lot where he had worked as a janitor years before.

It is the dream of most Hollywood actors to write and produce their own movies, and Kevin was actually doing it. I was a little bit in awe.

The second reason I didn't really want to join the throng of people who were fawning over Kevin and to try to make him my friend was that I felt that my detached admiration for him would actually *help* me play the delicate, awkward scenes I was scheduled to shoot with him in the next couple of weeks.

The first time I stepped onto the baseball field on Don Lansing's farm to shoot the final scenes from the movie, I felt like a rookie relief pitcher being called into the final game of the World Series. Most of the movie had been shot, and all I had to do was to throw a few good "pitches" and trust that my teammates would take care of the rest. There was an electricity in the air, because I was the new guy on the set and nobody knew whether I could pitch or not.

Even though it was still an hour before sunset, the crew was hustling around, setting up dolly track for the camera to roll on and preparing silk curtains to diffuse the light from the setting sun.

Close-up, the grass under my feet was unnaturally green and crunchy, like walking on Easter basket grass. The sod that had been laid by four local high school baseball teams to create the field over the long Fourth of July weekend had died immediately in the relentless Iowa heat. The L.A. Dodgers groundskeeper had advised the film crew to do what he does when patches of late-season grass die at Dodger Stadium: Paint it green. The art department had painted it green all right, with Hudson sprayers, and I was assured that the cameras couldn't tell the difference, but the "crunch" of the grass underfoot was a little unnerving.

Phil Robinson looked even more tired than the day before. The weight of the shoot was taking a toll on him. He spoke quietly and seemed to be avoiding eye contact. I was worried, too. I didn't want to tell anyone, but I still felt removed from the scene emotionally. Somehow, in the three months between the audition and the filming, my father's death had ironically blocked me from my feelings.

Even though I was permitted to hang out in my dressing room until they were ready for me, I wanted to be on the set, hoping that watching the crew set up for the scene would help me to get into character.

With emotional scenes, timing your feelings can be the most difficult part. Anyone who has been on a set knows that making movies is a waiting game. With scenes that are shot at magic hour, endless waiting turns instantly to "hurry up" mode because the window of perfect light is so short.

While the crew worked to get everything set up for the final scene, I slowly wandered away from the camera near the first base line, across the infield and outfield to the first row of tall corn in deep left field. I wanted a moment to myself to take it all in, before the pressure of the rolling cameras fought the setting sun.

On my left hand was my security blanket. I had been carrying it around all day. It was my father's mitt. There had been no opportunity to sneak its appearance into the movie so far—all the other players had already established their gloves and the prop department had given me a catcher's mitt to use in the final scene.

I had assumed that my father's recent death would make me extra emotional when it came time to shooting my scene with Kevin. So far, it had been hard to feel emotional about it, because I could not convince myself that my father was dead. Even though I had held his hand when he took his last breath, I could still feel his presence around me.

That was the truth of my situation. "Acting was not lying; it was telling the truth." *How could I feel my father's absence when he was still around me?*

I held my father's mitt in my hand and paced in front of the corn. They would be ready to shoot in a few minutes and I could feel that I was still empty inside. When I got to deep center field, I stopped at the edge of the corn. From here, the busy crew looked like a miniature work detail perfectly posed on one of my father's elaborate toy train displays, laying track for the camera dolly on the crunchy, manicured grass.

For a brief moment, the smell of the nearby creek drifted past my nose. I heard the breeze rattle the corn leaves. I looked around me. The sun was minutes from setting and, from here, with the tiny bleachers and the glowing farmhouse reflecting the setting sun in the background, it really did look like heaven.

I held my father's mitt up to my nose. This glove was probably sixty years old but I could still make out the faint scent of leather and Dad's saddle soap. I felt like a pitcher whispering to his mitt in the bottom of the ninth.

"Dad, I know you're still around. I need your help. I want this scene to be good and I need you to help me..."

"Pretty as a pitcher, ain't it?" The voice was loud and nasally. I jumped a bit. It was Don Lansing again. *Where had he* come *from?*

"Yeah, it sure is." I could feel the crew was almost ready to shoot. I needed to be alone right now. "Don, I have to—"

"I grew up here, y'know. That house's the only place I ever lived."

"Yeah, you mentioned that." He stood there awkwardly. "You're a lucky man."

"You betcha I am." We both stood there looking at the crew working in the distance, like two farmers watching their corn grow, only I was in a pin-striped baseball uniform trying to prepare for an important scene. The silence lingered.

"Don, I really have to—"

"Y'know, this film crew has been awful nice to me and my mom and my sisters, givin' us stuff—*Shoeless Joe* t-shirts and ball caps and what-not."

"Yeah, they gave me a lot of stuff, too."

"And I got to feelin' kinda bad that I don't got nothin' to give back to 'em and all."

"I'm sure they don't care abou—"

"So I made this here for you, to say 'thanks.'" From his back pocket he fished out a gold-colored baseball cap with the 'DeKalb' winged corn logo on the front. I recalled farmers wearing these promotional caps from my farm days in Ohio. He held it out to me proudly. "I wrote my name on it for you."

I took the cap from his rough hands. Across the bill of the hat, in ball-point pen, were the words "Don Lansing farm" scrawled in large, loopy cursive, made all the more shaky by the pen having had to stumble across the rows and rows of perfect stitching on the bill. "I wanted to write it nicer, but…" He looked like an embarrassed third-grader bringing home a school project.

"Thank you, Don. I love it." I leaned in and hugged him, pinning the arm that he had outstretched for a handshake, between us. I lingered in the awkward man-hug in the setting sun, his right arm pinned between us while his left arm hung stiffly at his side. I could tell he was uncomfortable but hugging his unyielding body right now was just what I needed.

"First team!" I heard the A.D.'s distant voice from next to camera. That was my cue.

I released Don and he stepped away from me, an awkward smile on his face. "Thanks," I said.

"Y'r welcome."

With my new gold cap in one hand and my father's mitt in the other, I hustled back to the world of the movie. Don disappeared back into the corn or into a tunnel he'd secretly dug somewhere in the outfield.

Once I realized how to use my father's lingering presence instead of his absence to feed my emotions, I was able to treat each night's filming of the scene as another opportunity to let my dad know I loved him. Some evenings I found him in the sunset. Sometimes in the smell of the soil, or the chirp of the crickets or the breeze in the corn.

One of my favorite aspects of Phil Robinson's script for the movie is that the "rules" of the magical field are not fully understood. When Ray observes his brother-in-law Mark walk right through the middle of a game on the field, nearly getting hit by a pitch, without seeing the players at all, he says, "This is getting interesting." When Moonlight Graham walks to the edge of the field to help Karin, everyone can feel that some "rule" is about to be violated, but nobody knows exactly what will happen.

Ray tells Annie that the catcher is his father "before he was worn down by life", but when he introduces Annie and Karin, he stops short, saying instead, "This is... John."

I don't know if it reminded me of my childhood and my own father's reluctance to talk about his past, but I loved that Ray and John both know that they are father and son but neither say it, perhaps out of fear that saying it out loud will somehow break the magical "spell" they are both under and that John might disappear back into the corn forever.

Some of you who know the movie well may be thinking, *What about the part when Ray says,* "Hey, Dad, wanna have a catch?" When we shot the movie, there was no "Hey, Dad" in the script. It was just Ray saying "Hey!" followed by the cut to me turning around. During test screenings of the movie, a lot of the audience didn't understand why Ray doesn't tell his father who he is, so Kevin was invited to a "looping" stage (for post-production sound) to record the "Hey, Dad!" version, and it was inserted into the movie.

In the end, it didn't matter too much to me that it was added. It was much more important that there be no confusion that John is Ray's father. Besides, I got to have the fun of acting the "secret" relationship, and I think the "unspoken" version we shot contributed to the dynamic tension of the scene, even if it was changed in the final cut.

Kevin and I were curious about the use of the phrase "have a catch" instead of "play catch," as all the kids said it where I grew up in Ohio and where Kevin grew up in California. Director Phil Robinson told us that "have a catch" was his choice, because that was the phrase he used growing up on Long Island, New York.

Kevin was everything I hoped he would be. He was gracious and charming and serious about acting. He was generous and collaborative in the scene, which, in my experience, was not always the case with big stars.

We would block the scene with Phil and then walk off the set to let the camera crew do their work. Sometimes we would run lines or work out any rough spots in the scene with each other. It was his suggestion that we could both be rubbing callouses on our hands in the shot where we are first seen walking next to each other across the infield.

It was ironic that I was playing the father but still imagining Kevin as my own dad, but I had seen from my life that as I got older the roles of father and son became more fluid and tended to surge back and forth slowly, like a tide. The scene was a slightly different conversation every night, but I tried to make each magic-hour encounter with my "father" as treasured and truthful as I could.

The hardest part about shooting the final scene between Kevin and me was that the type of daylight that we needed for this scene was only available for a brief period each evening. We were shooting only during "magic hour," which is the fifteen-minute period just after sunset during which daylight is softer and has a more golden hue.

Although the scene only lasts for five minutes, it had to be shot many times from many different angles. We would shoot part of the scene with the camera on Kevin one evening, and then film my side of the conversation from the opposite angle the next. Since we could only shoot for fifteen minutes each evening, this meant that we had to shoot the scene over and over again for two weeks.

It was important to create the same level of soft-spoken intensity each night for two weeks in order for the scene to look like it was happening continuously on one magical night. All of my years onstage came in handy. On a couple of evenings, after preparing myself emotionally, it was decided that the sky had too many clouds in it to match what we had already shot and our scene was scrapped for the night.

As if he were playing his part, Phil Robinson, like my father, was not effusive with his praise after we completed a take. He would say, "That was fine. Let's do it again," without ever saying what he wanted done differently. All I could hear was my father's voice saying, "If at first you don't succeed..."

DON'T DROP THE BALL

"In theory there is no difference between theory and practice.
In practice there is."
-Yogi Berra

I only appear in the last five minutes of *Field of Dreams*. At the end of my small part in the film—the final scene of the movie— my character, John, has just accepted Ray's invitation to have a catch and, naturally, the script calls for us to do just that.

It is the climactic moment of the film, the moment that we've all been waiting for, the end of Ray's search and his Herculean labors, the easing of John's pain for his son's refusing to have a catch with him—in short, the Big Payoff.

At this point in the film, all the other storylines have been wrapped up: Shoeless Joe Jackson has had his chance to play baseball again, Dr. Archibald "Moonlight" Graham has finally had his chance to bat, Terence Mann has taken his opportunity to see what's beyond the corn, and it appears that Ray's farm will be saved from foreclosure by the baseball fans who "will most definitely come."

So to give the climactic moment the necessary gravitas, the director, producers, and the director of photography envisioned a stunning helicopter shot that would start on Ray and John playing catch on the field and slowly rise higher and higher until you see the headlights of hundreds of cars coming to the field.

To make matters slightly more difficult, the shot had to be done within a small window of twilight. Since the tighter shots of us playing catch had already been filmed at "magic hour," the sky had to be light enough to match those shots, yet dark enough to be able to clearly see the headlights of the cars approaching the field.

To accomplish this feat, the production manager Brian Frankish had hired two of the best in the business: helicopter "picture" pilot Davy Jones was renowned for his ability to fly sideways and keep the rotor out of the shot as he had done in the remake of *King Kong*, and John M. Stevens, who would be the man hanging out of the side of the helicopter strapped to a several hundred pound camera rig, trying to frame the perfect shot, steady the camera, avoid seeing the helicopter and, of course, keep from falling out.

On top of these concerns, the production needed volunteers to drive their cars in the final scene. In an era before computer-generated graphics, this was a major undertaking. Frankish and his production hero, Sue Reidel, decided to run an ad in the newspapers and on radio stations to invite local citizens with cars to come and be coordinated into positions along three miles of roads, zig-zagging from downtown Dyersville to the Lansing farm.

The first 3,000 respondents to the ad were invited to an all-day picnic at Dyersville Commercial Club Park. They ate barbecue and corn and eventually it was explained to them exactly what was expected of them that night and the care and precision and urgency with which they would be required to move. Just before they left to find their positions on the road, executive producer Brian Frankish opened his script and stood in front of the assembled extras. Through a bull-horn he read them Terrence Mann's speech about baseball, ending with:

"...It reminds us of all that once was good and could be again. People will come. People will most definitely come." As Frankish clicked off the bullhorn, the crowd of extras was silent for a long moment. Then they burst into cheers and moved excitedly to their cars. Gentlemen, start your engines...

Coordinating 3,000 extras in 1,500 separate cars was an even more daunting task than it appeared. It required the cooperation of the highway patrol and the local radio station, which broadcast the director's instructions to the extras in their vehicles through their car radios. Because the cars had to stay in line on the roadways for hours, porta-potties had to be provided at strategic positions that couldn't be seen by the camera. The local auto club was on hand to assist any vehicles that overheated or broke down. Trucks drove down the rows of cars delivering peanuts and popcorn along with ice and water to overheated drivers as well.

In order for the headlights to have the desired impact, a blackout was agreed upon for the Dyersville area. The local train schedule was interrupted and, because Dyersville is a baseball-friendly town, five other baseball diamonds agreed not to play their scheduled games that night.

This was, by far, the single most expensive and complicated shot in the movie, costing perhaps $5,000 a minute to shoot, and no one was sure they'd get a second chance at it, due to the constraints of the lighting and the logistics of organizing thousands of extras in their cars, the helicopter, the weather and the budget. Returning the next day to try again would be impossible.

Needless to say, there was a bit of pressure on the entire crew to synchronize all these elements, on top of their having just been made to move all the trucks and trailers, in fact the entire film company, to another location, to avoid being seen in a shot that would expose a few square miles of Iowa landscape.

Despite all these crazy considerations and the real challenges the director and producers and camera operators were facing with this climactic shot, I was concerned with only one small thing—dropping the ball.

I'm sure it sounds petty in comparison to the other more important things that could possibly go wrong, but for me to accidently drop the ball during a routine game of catch, during the million-dollar payoff shot of the movie was an embarrassment that I was not ready to face. And it was not without warrant.

I had always been a pretty good fielder, but I was nowhere near the ballplayer Kevin was. Casually playing catch a million times in my backyard with my brother was a far cry from playing catch with a star actor with 150 people watching your every move in addition to a helicopter filled with million dollar equipment. Especially with a giant leather bagel strapped to my hand.

For those of you who have never put your hand into a vintage catcher's mitt from the 1950's, like the kind my sweaty hand was now in, you wouldn't know that it is a completely inflexible piece of cowhide, padded to the degree that it is like trying to catch a baseball with a giant submarine sandwich. There is no way to grab the ball with the glove when it hits the pocket and it is almost impossible to even feel when the ball has hit the mitt, so thick is the padding. So my fear, however self-indulgent, was real.

Besides, this was to be my last shot in the movie. I was proud of my other scenes in the film and I didn't want to blow it all by dropping the ball now.

So, the moment finally arrived. After hours of set up and double-checking, preparation and waiting, the time was right. The volunteers were parked by the side of the road for miles in their cars, listening for instructions on their car radios and waiting for production assistants strategically positioned along the route who would wave frantically for everyone to turn on their lights and start driving slowly toward the field.

The helicopter, with Phil Robinson inside, was warmed up and getting ready for take-off, making any kind of verbal communication on the ground impossible and blowing the perfect infield grass into a churning, green sea of confusion. The cameraman was making final adjustments on the camera rig, and the light in the sky was finally perfect. My stomach was in knots. Lights. Camera. Play ball…

The helicopter idling in left field slowly ramped up its engine. The rush of wind created by its rotors was unexpectedly strong and I widened my stance and leaned into it a bit to avoid being pushed over. I don't know why it didn't flatten the corn next to the takeoff site. I wondered if the crosswind would affect our throws (I hoped Kevin wouldn't jokingly throw me a knuckleball in that maelstrom of wind).

No matter how many times you rehearse the "money shot," it is always an adrenaline rush the first time you do it with the cameras rolling. Everyone is wound a little tight from trying to anticipate every potential problem, but there are hundreds of decisions, from the lens selection to the flight path to the amount of light in the sky, that could turn a spectacular set-up into a mediocre finish.

In addition, all the department support teams that had been running around to set things up for rehearsal now had to be sequestered behind the house to avoid being seen in the widening shot as the helicopter lifts off.

Even the walkie-talkies that had been laid next to the pitcher's mound for rehearsal to tell us where to stand and when to start playing catch had to be removed to make sure they wouldn't be seen in the shot.

Not that we could have heard them anyway. There was no way to anticipate the roar of the spinning rotors that drowned out any attempt to communicate last minute instructions by walkie-talkie.

Luckily, the first take went smoothly. No one could be absolutely sure that the headlights from the line of cars were visible enough and so it was decided to try it one more time while there was still light in the sky. As the helicopter returned to left field, the AM radio station that was broadcasting to the 3,000 extras in 1,500 cars, instructed them to prepare themselves for a second take.

Cameras were reloaded and last minute adjustments were made, and everyone was moving as fast as they could to get ready for "Take Two." I was relieved that I hadn't dropped the ball the first time. Maybe my father's coaching me with his old glove as a child had finally come in handy. But I realized that, in case they couldn't use the first take, I had all the same pressure for take two.

I was amazed that the make-up department rushed out to powder our faces as usual between takes, even though the camera was never closer than fifty feet, and we were standing in a whirling helicopter "hurricane."

Everything was reset and the extras' cars on the driveway were finally back in position. "Action!" was screamed into the pilot's radio headset, the rotors roared and Kevin and I settled into another "windy" game of catch. Another smooth take was achieved, but word passed quickly through the deafening noise that the long line of headlights just wasn't making the impact that Phil and cinematographer John Lindley had hoped. The cars could be seen but it was agreed that, in the shot, it simply did not look like the vehicles were moving.

By now, the sky was almost completely dark and there was worry that a third take wouldn't match the preceding "sunset" shot of Kevin asking me for a game of catch. But no one wanted to end the shooting of this beautiful but difficult film with any shot that was less than perfect.

Phil had an idea. We would try one more take with a slight adjustment. If it didn't work out or it was too dark, he would have to use one of the other takes. But after all this work, stunted corn, dead grass and a near nervous breakdown, he had to give it a try.

As the crew hustled to reload the film in the camera and the extras, again, were asked to return to their original positions, they were given one further instruction by the voice on their car radios.

As the helicopter revved to start their third and final take and Kevin and I took this as our cue to start our third and final game of catch, the drivers of the cars were asked by way of their car radios to flash their high beams off and on to make it appear as if they were passing things along the road. No one had any idea if it would work.

"Rolling!" "Action!" I "pitched" my third game of the day. "Cut!"

And that was a "wrap."

The 3,000 extras were sent home, the cast and crew said their good-byes and, within a few days, the excitement of *Shoeless Joe* had vanished like a traveling circus and everything was back to normal on the Lansing farm. Phil, safely back in L.A., finally got to have his sushi.

The next day, when editor Ian Crafford looked at the developed film from the final pivotal night of shooting, it was discovered that the first two takes of the elaborate final shot had mysteriously come out completely black! Fortunately, the final take, with the flashing high beams, was perfect.

THE SCREENING

"We just don't recognize life's most significant moments while they're happening.
Back then I thought, 'Well, there'll be other days.'
I didn't realize that that was the only day."
\- Doc Graham from W. P. Kinsella's *Shoeless Joe*

Once *Shoeless Joe* wrapped and I returned home to Venice, California, my life went back to normal. I went on auditions, paid my rent, hung out with friends and performed in plays. While the editors were busy with the composer, director and producers getting the film into shape, I put it out of my mind. That is pretty typical in the film business. Because the average feature film takes over a year to edit and score, and actors are always looking for their next job anyway, it's easy to forget the one you already have in the can.

Besides, I told myself, it's only a small role at the end of a film that probably won't be seen by a lot of people anyway. It was too sweet and magical a film to be very popular, I reasoned, and, anyway, nobody goes to baseball movies, especially ones with obscure titles like *Shoeless Joe*. If I got all excited about it, I'd just be disappointed when it finally came out. So with my old Midwestern reasoning, I put the movie out of my mind.

Meanwhile, after ten months of editing, Phil Robinson was still worried that his dream movie was going to be a flop. All the compromises caused by the drought and scheduling problems had left him with a film that was very little like the one he had imagined when he first fell in love with the novel *Shoeless Joe.*

One day, Universal Studios executive Tom Pollock called Phil into his office and informed him that the title of the film *Shoeless Joe* was going to be changed to *Field of Dreams.* This was the last straw—Phil was mad. *Field of Dreams*?! he thought. *It sounded like the name of room deodorizer.*

Phil argued against the change. Pollock was firm. He explained that test audiences had been confused by the title, thinking it was a movie about a homeless person. It would have to be changed.

Phil dreaded calling the novel's author Bill Kinsella to tell him the bad news. Finally, with the release of the film only months away, he called Kinsella and apologized about the new title. He explained that he had fought for *Shoeless Joe* but that Universal was adamant about changing it.

Kinsella demurred. "It's okay," he said. "*Shoeless Joe* wasn't my title anyway. The publisher chose it when they released the book." Phil, who had worked intimately with the book for six years, was shocked by this revelation.

"What was *your* title?" Phil asked.

"*Dream Field.*"

In March of 1989, I got a letter from Shoeless Joe Productions, stating that they had scheduled a cast and crew screening of the movie, now called *Field of Dreams,* for March 30th in a large screening room at MGM (now Sony) studios. It was typical to have a screening for all the people involved with the film prior to the release date for the general public. These events are usually a lot of fun: a chance to catch up with people you had laughs with during filming, but probably haven't seen since. Everyone is in a good mood, reliving the exploits and embarrassments that occurred on set and promising again to stay in touch.

There is usually a tense moment, after the director does his introduction and welcome in front of the screen, and the lights finally fade to indicate the start of the film, when everyone's breath collectively gets shallower and they brace for what they are about to see.

The director, producers, editors and composer have been looking at the film all day, every day, for over a year, and they have lost all objectivity. They are dying to have someone else's opinion, but are sometimes afraid they have blown it. Camera operators are hoping their focus never went soft, production designers pray that the dead grass they had to paint green didn't look too fake, producers are wondering if they can get people to come see it, and actors, like me, are scared that we may look foolish or, worse yet, that we may have been cut from the film entirely. Everyone wants the movie to be good and we all want to be good in the movie. Needless to say, the insecurity in the room is palpable.

As we all sat in the theater watching, it was clear early on that we had no reason to worry. Phil had done a great job putting it together and everyone was beginning to relax. There were laughs in the right places and Kevin was finding the perfect balance of innocence and strength, that great sense of naïve humor that he does better than anyone. Everyone was relaxing as they let go of their own insecurities and went on the ride.

I was immediately aware how much James Horner's amazing musical score for the film was pushing me like a strong tailwind toward the final scene. It had started out slowly and quietly, with the delicate, magical chords that accompany the early cornfield voice, but now it had grown to a rumble like the thunder of an unexpected storm on the prairie, and it was pushing me faster and faster toward the culmination of Ray's dream.

I hadn't realized while reading the script or shooting the movie how much the film moves toward the final encounter between Ray and John. I had convinced myself that I only had a five-minute scene that ties up the last loose ends of the movie, not the climactic, emotional, archetypal redemption of Father and Son.

As I watched with disbelief, my face appeared forty feet tall on the screen. With the brilliant camera push-in to Kevin's amazing reaction to seeing his father as a young man for the first time, I was swept up in the emotion of it, just like everyone else in the room.

The air became thick as the weight of everyone's internal father squeezed into the crowded screening room and we all fought to see through brimming eyes just how this scene that we had all created a year before was going to play out.

The final minutes of the film seemed endless, as if they were played in slow motion. When Ray finally asked John to have a catch, there was hardly a dry eye in the house. As the camera soared up to reveal the line of cars approaching the field, a collective sigh of relief rose and applause exploded as the credits rolled.

As might be expected at cast and crew screenings, everyone diligently watched as the credits rolled, proud to see their own name scroll by and ready to applaud or yell out jokes as the names of beloved fellow crew members floated slowly to the ceiling, like angels whose work here was done. Fresh applause greeted Phil's final surprise dedication: "To Our Parents."

As the lights rose in the screening room, everyone expressed their relief and excitement. Unlike other screenings, where the movie did not realize the collective aspirations of the cast and crew, everyone was happy to make eye contact and pat each other on the back for a job well done and laugh at the trials and tribulations of the months spent in the Iowa wilderness.

No one was more surprised by the overall impact of the film, and the part I played in it, than I was. What had been a small role at the end of the shooting schedule had been transformed in post-production into a pivotal moment in the film and everyone was quick to pat me on the back and offer generous predictions for my future stardom.

Even Kevin, who was just months away from shooting his Oscar-winning classic *Dances With Wolves*, quietly told me that my climb to stardom was likely to take five years, as his had from the time of his small role in *Frances* to his bust-out explosion in *Bull Durham*. These were some of the many kind words Kevin would say to me over the years to come.

As we watched the screening that afternoon, I had seen my name appear in the opening credits of the movie instead of at the end of the film as had been negotiated, but, with all the other emotion and excitement in the room, I hadn't really taken it in. I found out later that the director, Phil Robinson, had given me a bump up in status on his own volition. It was a generous compliment that has always meant a lot to me.

In the midst of everyone's enthusiasm at the screening, I was told I should really get a publicist and I was given a few recommendations and phone numbers. As I thought about trying to take advantage of my role to further my career, though, I realized that there was a problem.

Any magazine article that I might be featured in would invariably want to know what role I played in the film. The easiest answer, "Kevin Costner's father," created confusion right away. How could I have played Kevin's father if I was a few years younger than him? If the article had attempted to explain that I came back at the end of the film as a young man, it would ruin the surprise that is the culmination of Ray's journey.

In fact, I realized that any mention of "Ray's father" as being an actual character in the film would be a spoiler that could potentially destroy the magic everyone had worked so hard to create. It would be very hard for anyone to write an article about my role in the film without revealing elements of the plot that would compromise future audiences' enjoyment of it.

In the end, I didn't end up hiring a publicist to maximize the impact of my small role in the film. Was my failure to do so really a desire to not spoil the surprise ending, or was it just knee-jerk Midwestern modesty?

Did I feel the pressure of finally getting what I had always wanted, and simply got scared?

I had seen how Kevin was surrounded by fans wherever we went in Dubuque. It seemed like exactly what I wanted, but I began to see that celebrity has its price to exact as well. Sometimes Kevin couldn't even finish telling a story without being interrupted by a starstruck fan.

Did I sabotage my dream on purpose, just when realizing it was finally in my grasp?

I know who you are." He was an older man, well-dressed but in clothes that had seen too many years. Tweed suit. Vest. Nice, but a little dirty. "I'm sorry, are you talking to me?" I straightened the stack of theatre programs in my hand.

"Actor, right?" He looked up at me, his ice-blue eyes melting behind loose eyelids.

"That's right."

He nodded slowly, congratulating himself. "I knew it. Yes, sir."

I was busy, but I didn't want to be rude. "How do you know me?"

He was still nodding. "The father. *Field of Dreams,* right?"

"That was me." No response. I needed to move on if I expected to pick up the rest of the discarded programs before the next show started. "Are you a baseball fan?" I asked.

"No, not much. Loved to play catch, though."

"Me, too."

"I used to play catch with my son when he was little. He got to be a pretty good ballplayer. You look a little like my Scotty. That's how I recognized you." He eyed the programs in my hand. "You look like you've got things to do…"

"No, nothing urgent." I sat down, leaving an empty seat between us. Picking up programs would have to wait.

"I lost my son Scott when he was a teenager, back in '92." I looked at his face, surprised by this sudden confession. He looked back at me calmly.

"I'm sorry," I said softly.

"Beg your pardon?"

"I said, 'I'm sorry' about your son." I had said it only a little louder, but it felt like I was yelling.

"Thank you." He paused a moment. "My father tried to comfort me, but I couldn't help but feel he blamed me a little bit, too. Maybe I imagined it. Hell, I blamed myself. It was a hard time for me."

"I can imagine..."

"Got a divorce. Pushed everyone away. Isolated myself in my pain. For years. Just sat at home and watched TV." His fingers moved independently as he talked as if he were playing an invisible trumpet.

"One night, that movie comes on. *Field of Dreams*. I couldn't follow it at first, maybe it was all the commercials. But I kept watching it. Finally, at the end, the father comes back, young again. Free from all his mistakes. I started crying, right there, alone in my room. I didn't think I had any tears left, but there they were. I think I was really crying for myself." His watery eyes looked at me keenly, as if through time. "You look like him." He reached with his flittering hand and it landed on mine. He smiled.

"The next day, I decided to start over. Give myself a second chance. I thought, *I want to be a young man again, too*. Like you. Start over. But I didn't know what to do. I forgot how to be young. *What did I do back then that made me happy?*

"So I drove to my father's house and asked him if he'd play catch with me. He looked at me like I was crazy—he was 81 at the time. But it turned out he had seen the movie on TV the previous night, too."

"Really?"

"Yes, sir. Go figure... So I dug out our old gloves and a ball and we threw the ball back and forth in the back yard like we did when I was a boy. Well, not as far or as fast, but Dad could still throw and I could still catch." He smiled and patted my hand with his.

"We didn't say much, but the sun was shining, the grass was a little wet and it felt good to be young again."

MEN DON'T CRY

"That's the thing about pain," Augustus said, and then glanced back at me.

"It demands to be felt."

- John Green, *The Fault in Our Stars*

The second weekend after *Field of Dreams* was released in April of 1989, I got a call from Phil Robinson, inviting me to go see the movie with him and producer Chuck Gordon in Westwood, near the UCLA campus, where it was playing. I was flattered to have been asked, but I had to perform that night in a play in Hollywood and told him I was unable to go.

I thought it was sweet that they wanted to watch the movie again. Usually, by the time a movie is finished, the director and producer have watched every part of it hundreds of times in the editing room and at various screenings, and no matter how good it is, there is very little desire to sit through it again.

"Haven't you and Chuck seen enough of this film, Phil?" I asked cautiously.

"We don't watch the film," he said simply, "we watch the audience. We just show up for the last five minutes. You should try it."

"What am I looking for?"

"You'll know. Don't forget to stay for the credits."

"What do you mean?" I asked.

"Just do it."

Phil had a way of talking that made me feel like I was the most special person on the planet. Even though our conversation had happened on the phone, I could tell Phil had hung up with a smile on his face. I wondered why he had been so amused. I had already thanked him at the cast screening for raising my status in the credits of the movie and we had all told him how much we loved his "For Our Parents" tribute just before the film fades to black. *Had he done something else to the film?*

I was still thinking about it hours later, as I prepared to go onstage in the second act at a small storefront theater across the alley from a hip Hollywood restaurant. I finally laid down my script in the tiny, cluttered dressing room and walked quietly backstage to coax my thoughts into the alternate world of the stage I was about to enter. For a brief second, my mind flashed on the absurdity of what I was about to do.

Here I was, standing silently in the dark behind a flimsy, black curtain, listening to the other actors only a few feet away performing their parts. Although they couldn't see me, I could hear the audience, also in the dark, moving in their seats and I could feel the energy of their attention to what was happening on stage.

I was waiting, dressed as an English sea captain, and I could faintly hear dishes being washed across the alley, and busboys joking in Spanish as they played their parts and I waited to play mine.

At that moment, I felt like a child hiding behind the living room curtains, listening to my parents talking, hearing things I'm not supposed to hear, frozen-in-place excited to hear that breathy, mumbled laughter and scared to death that I'd be found out.

In another moment, I would "become" someone else. I would walk out from behind that dark curtain into the bright light and I would attempt to entertain people I'd never met by pretending to be someone who never existed. I would speak words that were written by someone else, somewhere else, words that I had rehearsed hundreds of times, in hundreds of different ways, in an effort to say them in the "perfect" way that would make the people watching in the dark perhaps understand their lives a bit more or at least to laugh or cry a bit.

These strangers in the dark would judge me for my efforts and, I hoped, reward me for how convincingly I'd fooled them, by hitting their hands together repeatedly. I would thank them for their applause by bending over at the waist and standing back up again. Then we, the audience and the actors, would all leave the dark theater and go home, or go out, or go on to our next role in our performance of our lives.

Then I heard my cue and walked onstage.

After the show, several audience members came backstage to see friends who were in the show, and now that the illusion was over, they were allowed to peek behind the curtain. I was introduced and congratulated and was welcomed back into the "real" world with talk of how bad the traffic was that night on Sunset Boulevard. After shedding my costume and make-up, I left the theater through the stage door, waved to the busboys, who were hosing down the alley, and climbed into my car.

As I drove through Westwood toward my apartment in Venice, it was almost 11:30. Although I had missed the 8:00 showing of *Field of Dreams* that Phil invited me to, it occurred to me that the later showing might be just about over. On a whim, I turned right onto Westwood Boulevard and luckily found a parking spot across from the Avco Theater.

The stern woman in the box office told me that there were only about 15 minutes left and that the screening had been sold out.

"I only need to stand in the back and watch the credits," I offered.

"You might disrupt the other patrons," she intoned, without looking up from her dog-eared paperback.

"I'll be very quiet. I promise."

"What is so interesting about the credits?"

"I don't know exactly. That's why I need to see them. I'm happy to pay." She pretended to study her screening schedule. I felt too embarrassed to pull the "I'm *in* this movie" card, so I just stood there, looking hopeful. "Please. I promise not to be disruptive." I held out my money and, grudgingly, she took it.

I walked through the bright lobby and into a different dark theater this time. It was crowded, and the air was heavy with the breath of six hundred warm bodies silhouetted against the bright screen. It looked for a moment as if the audience itself were sitting in a cornfield. James Earl was walking toward the camera forty feet tall and waxing poetic about "baseball," exploding his "b's" like each syllable was a firework of hope. I smiled to myself.

"People will come, Ray. People will most definitely come."

As my eyes adjusted to the darkness, I found a single empty seat on the aisle in the second to last row and quietly sat down. I was immediately drawn in to the film by the audience around me.

I watched as Moonlight Graham became Doc Graham and saved Karin's life. I watched as the ballplayers made their way to the corn and Terrence Mann promised to write about it.

Finally, Shoeless Joe says "If you build it…he will come" and magically I found myself watching myself on the big screen in a dark sea of strangers.

When Ray says, "It's my father," there was an audible, collective gasp in the theater and the tall man next to me put his hand over his mouth. I watched the rest of the film with tears in my eyes, watching the audience watch the film. The silence in the large room was uncanny. It felt as if everyone in the entire auditorium was holding their breath.

"You wanna have a catch?" The tall man next to me sank down in his chair and put both of his hands over his face.

"I'd like that." Muted sobbing broke out in small groups all around me. The man watched Ray and John play catch through his fingers, the movie screen reflected in the tears on his cheek.

I watched as the credits began to roll and the first few members of the audience got up to leave. Many had clearly been crying and I wanted to be invisible. It felt wrong to be there, like I had wandered into a stranger's funeral. I hunched down into my seat.

The tall man was leaning away from me onto his wife and she was comforting him earnestly. I couldn't stop watching his heaving shoulders out of the corner of my eye and strained to hear what they were whispering to each other.

I felt like a strange voyeur of grief. I was desperate not to be recognized, for fear it would break the spell, but I wanted also to comfort them. I knew what it felt like to lose a father. I felt both proud and humbled to be there. As they stood up, I put my hand over my face but watched them leave, sniffling and holding each other as the credits rolled on.

There were a lot of people still in their seats. Many of these groups were men—large, athletic men who I imagined had come with their buddies to watch a movie about baseball. Now they were crying and couldn't stop. I watched one group of five men in UCLA jerseys that never said a word to each other. They sat next to each other, crying, in their own separate grief, getting comfort only from the darkness and the fact that they weren't weeping alone.

Another group of four slightly older men were seated with their arms on each other's shoulders as if they were in a huddle at a touch football game. They were crying and occasionally thumping each other's backs.

A young man was turned sideways in his seat and hugged an older man next to him, weeping uncontrollably. I imagined they were a father and son. I had a pang of longing, regretting that I would never have the opportunity to watch the movie with my dad.

When the final credit "For Our Parents" finally faded from the screen and the music score ended, there were still several of these groups left in their seats. Only when the house lights slowly came up to reveal them, were these men able to pull themselves together and make their way slowly toward the exits.

As the young men in the usher crew avoided eye contact and worked through the aisles to clean up the mess, I walked out through the lobby into the cool, spring night.

The next morning, I called Phil and left a message to thank him for inviting me to "watch the credits." It was truly a gift to feel the audience's reaction firsthand. I've never had another experience like it.

I hoped that Phil could feel that I was smiling as I hung up.

SACRED CORN

"When a father gives to his son, both laugh; when a son gives to his father, both cry."

– William Shakespeare

N*ew York Times* reviewer Caryn James predicted on the day the film opened: "Audiences will probably believe Mr. Costner's illusion or not, love or hate this film. It seems much easier to fall into *Field of Dreams* than to resist its warm, intelligent, timely appeal to our most idealistic selves."

Roger Ebert wrote: "*Field of Dreams* is the kind of movie Frank Capra would have made and Jimmy Stewart might have starred in."

Bill Simmons, a sports columnist, went further: "I've always felt there were two types of people: Those who love *Field of Dreams* and those who have no soul."

But there were detractors. *Rolling Stone's* Peter Travers called it the "worst movie of 1989."

I think that the audience for *Field of Dreams* could be divided into two groups: those like Ray, Annie, Karin and Terence Mann, whose hopeful natures allow them to see the "invisible" players on the field, and those like his logical brother-in-law Mark, who could see only the empty field where someone should be growing corn.

Field of Dreams was nominated for three Oscars in 1989: Best Movie, Best Adapted Screenplay and Best Musical Score. *Driving Miss Daisy* won the first two categories and *The Little Mermaid* won for best score.

In 1992, "Is this heaven? No, it's Iowa," was adopted as Iowa's official state motto.

As a tribute to the lasting legacy of a film shot 24 years earlier, for the 2013 baseball playoffs, the network and Major League Baseball chose to shoot their broadcast intro at the *Field of Dreams* movie site, featuring silhouetted players coming out of the corn to play the game.

When the director Phil Robinson decided to build the field on the flat land just west of Don Lansing's farmhouse to maximize the late day sunlight, the field extended onto a neighbor's farm. The fence the production company removed between the two properties fell just behind the third base line. Right and center fields were on Al and Rita Ameskamp's property.

The following spring when planting time came, before the movie had even been released, Don decided to take part in a government crop reduction program and to leave the baseball field intact, "in case it became legendary." Al decided to plow under his outfield grass and plant corn.

On May 5th, 1989, the first visitor arrived at Don Lansing's farm, just two weeks after the film was released. He was driving from New York to L.A. and wanted to see the field "before they tore it down." He left Don his prized N.Y. Giants ballcap as a memento.

The next year, the Ameskamps returned their outfield to grass and, in the following years, the field eventually saw 65,000 visitors per summer from every state and dozens of foreign countries. There are over a hundred guestbooks, each with thousands of names and remarks about the emotional experiences they had at the field.

Sons brought their fathers and fathers brought their sons. Brothers who had not seen each other in twenty years arrived at the field on the same day. A middle-aged man knelt and cried over home plate for his lost son. A couple was married there in 1990. Don Lansing himself proposed to his wife Becky a few months after she came to the field on a snow-covered New Year's Eve in 1994, following a dream she'd had a month earlier at her home in Colorado.

It is estimated that well over a million people have visited the field since the movie came out in 1989.

It is unfortunate that the baseball field was placed across a shared property line, but nobody imagined when the field was built that life would imitate art so profoundly. Much has been made by the media over the divided field and the "feud" between the Lansings and the Ameskamps. To tell that story fairly would require a book in itself. But it, too, is an American story, one of greed and good intentions, privacy and property rights but, mostly of all parties wanting to be a part of an American dream that one day dropped from the sky onto the cornfield between their two farms.

Both the book *Shoeless Joe* and the movie *Field of Dreams* proposed that the farmer should charge visitors for the opportunity to come to the field, "for it is money they have, and peace they lack." Don and Al have taken care of their farms for the past 25 years, mowing and maintaining the field, paying for insurance and letting people wander around their properties, all without ever charging them an admission fee.

Both farmers erected souvenir stands, but neither ever allowed a fast food concession or advertising banner or any of the other manifestations of American consumerism that, as Terence Mann laments in the movie, have "rolled across this country like an army of steamrollers."

Al Ameskamp died in 2004 and Rita sold their farm back to Don Lansing, for hundreds of times more than what Al's father had purchased it from Don's uncle Lawrence for in 1967. Don turned 72 this year and he still oversees the maintenance of his family farm, even though the property now has new owners.

It is surprising that, for the overwhelming popularity of the movie site as a tourist destination there is refreshingly little to actually "do" there. People come, they walk around, they have a catch and some good old-fashioned fun, but mostly, they reminisce.

One entry from a 2004 guestbook says it best. The writer clearly intended their words as the greatest compliment, but it carries a double meaning;

"It doesn't take much to be a tourist attraction in Iowa."

Being a professional actor, like being a professional athlete, can sometimes feel like being in the lottery. You can be cast or not cast for a thousand different reasons, many of which are out of your control. There is a random quality to it that can be both invigorating and infuriating. Although I have continued to work in Hollywood, with my small role in *Field of Dreams*, I won the lottery. I have received a little of what every person wants and deserves—recognition for doing what they love to do.

Although Joseph Jefferson "Shoeless Joe" Jackson died seven years before I was born, our lives seem to have been destined to be linked. The first television job I ever got (1981) was called *The Trial of Shoeless Joe Jackson*. It was a locally-produced (Chicago) CBS special that dramatized the Black Sox Scandal. I played sports reporter Ring Lardner.

Then, in the summer of 1987, I went back to Chicago to visit my friend Bill Payne. While in town, I decided, on a whim, to visit my former agent and friend Ann Geddes at her office in the Hancock Building. After a nice visit, as I was about to leave, another of her clients, John Cusack, stopped in with an actor I'd never met, D.B. Sweeney.

John excitedly told Ann that, in preparation to play his role of Buck Weaver in the upcoming production of *Eight Men Out*, he had been granted permission to shag some flies and run bases on the field at Comiskey Park, where the real "Shoeless" Joe had played seventy years earlier. He asked me if I wanted to come along.

So before the movie *Field of Dreams* was even a twinkle in Universal Studios' eye, I got to play baseball with the actor (D.B.) who would portray Shoeless Joe Jackson in a movie (*Eight Men Out*) about the real events of Jackson's life and catch fly balls hit to me by "Shoeless Joe" in left field on the actual ground where the real Jackson had once played.

A year later, *Eight Men Out* was released, two years later *Field of Dreams* came out, and three years later the White Sox moved to the new stadium they built right across 35th Street from the old Comiskey, on Chicago's South Side.

When I was a freshman in high school, my friend Jim Kelly stood next to me in the locker room while I scanned the names of the players chosen for the baseball team and watched the disappointment dawn on my face when my name was not there. He reminded me recently that I had told him that day that the coach "would regret his decision to cut me from the team and that someday my picture would be in the Hall of Fame."

On a recent visit to Cooperstown, New York, he was surprised to see, hanging with other photos from baseball movies, the picture from *Field of Dreams* of Ray introducing his father to his wife and daughter. It was mostly a shot of my back and, if you hadn't seen the movie, you might not even recognize it as me, but there I was, wearing a pin-striped baseball uniform, hanging in the Baseball Hall of Fame.

It may not have been what I had meant when I said it, but life is not a movie and reality doesn't always work out exactly the way we dream it will.

As a result of my role in the film, I have been honored to help other people try to make their own dreams come true. I have been invited to appear at everything from board meetings to birthday parties. I was flown to Belfast, Ireland by Kent State grad student Michael Whitely, to dedicate a peace fountain he had built there. I have signed autographs and baseballs and photos and have donated items to charities.

All of these wonderful charities and foundations were at one point just a crazy idea in someone's head (like writing a story about a farmer who builds a baseball field, like a writer who turns it into a movie, like a boy who wants to save the world by becoming an actor).

Dreams don't happen without some work. The Voice from the movie doesn't say: "If you *think about* it, or *wish for* it, or *dream about* it, he will come." It says, "If you **build** it, he will come."

Some dreams are crazier than others.

In 2012, my agent forwarded me an email from a successful businessman in Pittsburgh named Ty Ballou who "had a business proposition for me." He was an alumnus of Northern Illinois University and wanted to do something fun to enhance the relationship of the University with their host city of Dekalb. Because DeKalb was, for many decades, the corn capital of the world, his plan was to build a 150-foot corn tower next to a museum and guest center in an area between the campus and the downtown area.

The tower would be in the shape of an ear of corn, complete with a circular staircase inside and a viewing platform on top, to look out at the university, the city of DeKalb, and the surrounding fields of, what else, corn.

He prepared a power-point presentation for the city manager and the university's board of trustees, including scenes from the film introduced by him. At the end of the clip of Kevin and me playing catch, I was to walk through the door of the conference room in a baseball shirt and tell them about my life on a farm and my dream of becoming an actor and my role in the film.

I accepted the offer, and flew out to play my part. Of course, my presence was a secret and I had to hide out before the meeting in the first floor bathroom, sometimes ducking into an empty stall if I heard someone approaching.

Once all the trustees were safely in the conference room, I stood in the hallway of the NIU administration building with my ear against the door to listen for my cue to enter. Employees walking in the hall did their best to ignore the strange man in the pin-striped baseball shirt lurking around the conference room with his ear to the door. For one secretary, who looked like she might call for security, a simple wave of my hand seemed to quell her suspicions. Only after she smiled at me did I realize how ridiculous I must have looked waving with my father's old baseball mitt on my hand.

In that moment, I was struck by the strange places my small role in this movie had taken me. When I heard my cue, I opened the door and walked in and watched the serious faces of the trustees turn to astonishment and smiles. The plan for the museum and guest center was approved, although there were some reservations about the practicality of a 150-foot tall ear of corn.

December 27, 1990

Dear Mr. Brown,

We love the movie *Field of Dreams*. Your performance makes us cry every time we watch it. Our four year-old son Dylan loves it, too.

Every time I would play catch with him in our backyard last summer, he would insist on walking out of the cornfield behind our house and saying, "Hey, Dad, do you want to have a catch?" I would have to say, "I'd like that," before he'd play catch with me.

I know this is a strange thing to ask, but we would love it if you would come to Dylan's fifth birthday party on July 15th, 1991 at our home. I would pay for your plane ticket, of course, and any other expenses you might incur. Although it's still six months away, we wanted to give you plenty of time to think about it and make arrangements if you wanted to come.

Yours truly,
Dave, Debbie and Dylan

SONS BECOMES FATHERS

"When we die, one by one,
(Oh my God, we leave like we come),
Like children, we'll run,
Far and free."
- Ted Lennon, from the song *Jesus Underwater*

W hen I got the letter on the previous page, I wrote the family and thanked them for their invitation, but told them that I wouldn't be able to make it. By the time June rolled around, though, I was still thinking about little Dylan and feeling a little guilty.

I thought it might be pushing my personal agenda of helping people realize their dreams a little too far to fly three-quarters of the way across the country for a kid's birthday party, but I had a feeling I should be at this party and my experience with the movie had made me a believer in listening to my intuition.

It also turned out that I was going to be in Ohio, helping with a fundraiser for my brother's local political campaign, within twenty minutes of the party's location. Was that just a coincidence or was it "meant to be?"

I had already told Dylan's father that I couldn't be there. And when people aren't expecting something to happen, the level of surprise multiplies exponentially. I love surprising people. I got this trait from my father, who taught us that everything tastes sweeter when you don't expect it.

With Dad's wisdom in mind, I pulled up to the non-descript house on the edge of the city limits and changed into the pin-striped jersey I had brought with me from a charity game at the *Field of Dreams* movie site. I wondered if I was making a grand mistake, coming to the party unannounced. The blue balloon tied to the mailbox hung limply, the breeze having wrapped its ribbon around the rusted iron scrollwork of the mailbox post like a drunken spider. I thought about taking this as an omen and heading home.

Before I let myself think about it too much, I opened the car door, grabbed my father's old-fashioned mitt for luck, and walked toward the house. I tucked the baseball I had autographed into my back pocket, ready to present to the birthday boy at just the right moment.

The smell of barbecue smoke floated past me. I heard faint voices and laughing from the back yard. I decided to take a peek back there, to see if there was a better way to stage this surprise visit. I walked casually around the left side of the house. Leaning against the rough, brick wall of the garage, I peered into the back yard like the advance scout on a raiding party.

I saw about a dozen adults milling about in a large, landscaped back yard, mostly around the barbecue, which stood close to the sliding glass back door. Six or seven kids, mostly boys about five, bounced on a trampoline with netting around the sides, fifty feet from the house, right where the grass of the back yard ended at a field of towering, green corn.

Mentally, I dropped into full "surprise planning" mode. I thought, if I could get myself, unnoticed, into that cornfield, I could give Dylan a birthday surprise he would never forget. I looked at the adjacent neighbors' properties and figured I could walk down the street a few houses, cut through a neighbor's yard into the corn, and double back to Dylan's house. *Boy, would he be surprised!*

I felt the excitement of anticipation in my stomach as I walked back to the street and looked for a quiet house I could walk past to get to the cornfield. I tried to make a mental note of how far I was walking so I would know how far to double back, once I got into the corn.

I found the perfect house and strode down the side yard confidently to minimize suspicion. I loved that these suburban houses had no fences around them. Unlike in Los Angeles, there was a welcoming sense here of no boundaries. I savored that feeling I had had as a child that I could just wander across yard after yard and never had to worry if I was trespassing.

As I walked confidently into the backyard, glancing at the unknowing birthday party revelers three backyards away, lost in my nostalgic reverie of my innocent childhood, a black German Shepherd leapt at me suddenly from the corner of my vision, barking wildly and flashing its sharp, white teeth. My heart leapt into my throat as I braced for the teeth to rip into my arm. I squealed loudly and brutally like a zebra being dragged down by a charging lion.

In a micro-second of my panic, I saw the headline: "Hollywood Actor Killed by Dog While Robbing Suburban Home." I wondered what Mom would think. By the time my thoughts returned to me, I realized the crazed dog was inside the house, blocked from me by the sliding glass doors closed between us.

Fully adrenalized now, I jogged away from the doors toward the cornfield, hoping that I could reach the corn before the owners of the home came running to see what had startled the dog. As I covered the last few yards, I glanced over at Dylan's party to make sure they hadn't been alerted by the still-bellowing police dog. Then, like Shoeless Joe in the movie, I disappeared into the corn.

If you have ever walked through a field of corn that is over your head, you know that it can be a disorienting experience. It can feel like a house of mirrors in which you can never quite trust what you are looking at and depth perception becomes a little dicey.

I was sure I was walking way too far. It occurred to me that instead of being mistaken for a robber and eaten by a dog, it might be more appropriate if my untimely death fell under the headline: "Field of Dreams Actor Lost In Cornfield."

Finally I began to hear the voices of children giggling on the trampoline and I followed them until I knew I was in the perfect position. I brushed off my jersey, which was now covered with pollen, dust and cobwebs from the corn. I crouched between the rows and tried to figure out the best way to choreograph my appearance.

The trampoline was only twenty feet away. I stood up and called in the deepest, whisper voice I could muster, "If you build it…" I paused for effect, "…he will come."

I looked through the leaves. No reaction. I tried again, a little louder. "If you build it…he will come." I looked again. I saw two of the small boys on the trampoline look my direction, their tiny brows knit.

"If you build it…he will come," I said once again. Now all the children had frozen and were looking into the cornfield. Suddenly, one of the boys' faces started to crumple and he yelled over his shoulder toward the barbecue, in a stiff, panicked voice, "Daddy!"

Uh oh, I thought. I hadn't figured that my little surprise might scare the kids.

The tone of his pleading voice simultaneously stiffened the spine of every parent in the back yard and all heads turned toward the trampoline like a startled herd of impala at a watering hole. Moms made their first steps toward the panicked voice and I knew I had to finish this thing quickly.

I took a deep breath and walked out of the corn.

For an instant, the people who watched me suddenly appear out of the empty cornfield, recoiled as if to run away. Then there was a moment of questioning looks that broke instantly into disbelief. Several of the boys stood with their mouths open.

One of the men at the grill started walking toward me, smiling enormously and reassuring the others, "It's him. The father from *Field of Dreams*. Oh my gosh…I can't believe you came!" The other adults seemed to exhale in unison. The kids on the trampoline were still frozen, confused by this 180-degree turn of events. The smallest boy, who was wearing a Cleveland Indians jersey, looked sick to his stomach. Wisps of his blond hair were standing straight up on his head from the static electricity of the trampoline. His brown eyes were as wide as satellite dishes. I knew at once that this was Dylan.

I kept my eyes on him as the man from the grill, who was also wearing an Indians jersey, held out his hand and I shook it. "I'm Dave. I thought you couldn't make it?"

"Surprise," I said softly. I walked slowly toward Dylan on the trampoline, watching him closely like I was approaching a startled animal. I didn't want him to lose it now and be scarred for life. "Dylan?"

He didn't answer, but his lip quivered and I knew he was about to lose it in front of all of his friends, at what was supposed to be the happiest moment of his young life. I racked my brain to think of the distracting comments I had used on my nephews when they were young and were about to fall apart. I couldn't think of anything. I walked right up to the trampoline.

"You wanna have a catch?" I asked Dylan.

His giant brown eyes blinked and when they opened, they were filled with tears. *Oh shoot, now I've done it…*

As I turned toward Dave for help, Dylan ran toward me on the lightly bouncing trampoline, threw his arms open and tried to hug me through the mesh of the trampoline's curtain. He was crying openly now and whispering through the mesh and his tears, "Thankyouthankyouthankyouthankyouthankyou..."

With Dylan stuck to me through the mesh, I moved the few feet to the opening flap and he dove through it and wrapped his arms around my neck tightly, wrapping his legs around my waist and wiping his drippy face on the side of my head. His body was warm and sweaty from the trampoline and the excitement of the surprise, but somehow, he smelled delicious, like a fresh loaf of bread.

The adults crowded around, smiling, introducing themselves and proudly pointing out their children on the trampoline. Without warning, Dylan wiggled out of my arms and disappeared into the house. I was chatting with his father when Dylan appeared at my feet, his oversized mitt and a baseball in his hand, and a look of anticipation on his face.

I ended up playing catch with him and with almost everyone at the party and posing for dozens of photos, but after a while, as I've found with almost all of my *Field of Dreams* encounters, once we've touched the emotion that the movie has inspired, everything else feels like small talk and it quickly gets awkward, like being a teenager left alone in a room with your friend's father.

I gave Dylan his autographed baseball and said my goodbyes. As I shook his hand, I could see in Dave's eyes that he wanted something more from me. I imagined that he wished I weren't an actor playing a part—he wanted me to *be* John Kinsella. At that moment, I wanted to be John, too—a fictional character, magically appearing from the dead, that could take him back through that magical cornfield, back to that perfect moment of his childhood, of all of our childhoods, when we stood at sunset, with the smell of fresh-cut grass in our noses and the rising chill of the dew on our arms.

We would play catch on the green grass or swim in the cool creek or recite Bible verses in front of a smiling congregation without a thought about the days that would have to follow.

OPUS/ by Berkeley Breathed

The Place Where
Dreams Come True

"Time is the longest distance between two places."
- Tennessee Williams, *The Glass Menagerie*

In 2005, I was surprised to see a Sunday comic with a picture of Kevin and me in it from *Field of Dreams*. It was a funny comic in the strip "Opus" lamenting that in spite of the idealized father and son in the final scene of the movie, we all go through life with the father we've got. In another of what has become an endless series of "coincidences" between my life and the movie's, it was published in newspapers across the country on my birthday.

The author of the cartoon was Pulitzer Prize-winner Berkeley Breathed, and like many of his strips, beyond the humor there is real truth—"Ya go to life with the dad you have."

As men, we are told we have to make our mark in the world. We are encouraged to dream big and to follow those dreams aggressively. The big winners in life are those who refuse to be denied and stay doggedly focused on their goals.

At the same time, we are told that we must provide for our families and sacrifice for them. When we try to do both of these things effectively, it is hard not to fall short in one or both. Regret is inherent in the deal.

Of course, I was not to blame for my father's thwarted dreams—he had made his own choices, even if some of those decisions were shaped by his experience of the Great Depression, World War II and the harsh choices his father had made. But, sometimes, as fathers, we tend to focus on the things we didn't do well rather than on the things we did do well. After all, who are we without something to "fix?"

About a year after my father died, my mother sold the farm we had grown up on. It was a huge house and a lot of land for just one person and my mother was relieved to move to a smaller house in town. When I came home to visit her the next year, I drove by the old house and noticed the changes the new owner made to it: new paint, a garage, a concrete drive-way and, finally, aluminum siding to cover the old wood shingles.

It was sad to watch changes being made to something I had invested so much of my young life working on, but I had to admit the new owner was doing a good job.

One day, I knocked on the door and explained that I had grown up in the house and would love to take a look inside. The new owner was gracious.

Many of the things my father and we had worked so hard on were undone. Dad's hand-built cabinets, the staircase, the pantry that held the Fer-Ri-Bar Farm candy store—all changed. I smiled at the new owner, a young carpenter, and told him how nice the place looked. And it did.

But I couldn't help feeling like my father's life had been erased. Even the Firestone plant where he had spent 23 years working was shut down and the tire business moved to Japan. What did this say about the value of my father's life, the legacy of his dreams?

How was it that the hard work, the lives, the dreams of men like my father were forgotten and paved over by that "army of steamrollers," as Terence Mann calls them in *Field of Dreams*, for the sake of progress? It didn't seem fair.

No one else will ever know my father. His meticulous measurements scribbled on the back of the drywall we nailed up forty years ago will forever live in the darkness between the wall studs. No one will ever know about his dream of remodeling a run-down farmhouse, because that farmhouse now looks like a cookie-cutter tract home, complete with a two-car garage and aluminum siding.

As I drove back to my mother's apartment in town, I finally realized that my father's dream had not been to remodel a farmhouse but to create a place where he could raise a family in the way he had always wanted for himself. One where he could prove that he was not *his* father by always being present in our lives.

I prefer to think that if my father was going to choose his family over his ambitions, he was going to get his money's worth out of us. He chose a farm that would isolate us from the worries of the world, so he could have us to himself. He picked a house where he could experiment with the architectural design concepts he had learned about in college. He picked a ramshackle house where even the work of inexperienced laborers like us, working right alongside him, would be a vast improvement over its current condition.

He created a household where, even though there wasn't much money, there was always enough for family vacations and where even simple things, like having a garden or going outside to the toilet, were turned into an unforgettable adventure. He made it possible for his three kids to pursue their dreams in a way he had never been able to.

My next movie after *Field of Dreams* was a thriller called *The Nanny*.

I had intended to turn down the film because of its scary content, but was convinced by my agents and manager that it was a wonderful opportunity: it was a studio movie, directed by an Academy award-winning director, it was the male lead, and I was offered the part without having to audition. I was also being offered more money to do it than all the other jobs I had ever done combined.

I told myself that this was just another stepping stone to getting bigger parts in better movies. I really enjoyed playing a lead role and I was proud of my work in the movie. The finished film, called *The Guardian* (**not** the 2009 film with Kevin Costner and Ashton Kutcher), was not very successful and I learned that sometimes it's better to have a small part in a good movie than a big part in a bad movie.

I didn't go on to be a movie star the way Kevin had predicted for me. That is no one's fault but my own. I've certainly second-guessed some of my decisions over the years in choosing agents and projects and in failing to promote myself when I had opportunities. Perhaps my hidden fears led me away from the things I told myself I wanted and maybe my dreams changed as I got closer to making them a reality.

It is easy to regret some decisions, and although *The Guardian* wasn't everything I wanted it to be, the money I made from the shoot allowed me to put a down payment on my first house—a small fixer-upper on two acres above a lazy creek about seventy miles north of L.A. Fixing it up was a lot of work (I tore out walls, put in hardwood floors, moved doors and added porches), but it ended up being a magical place to raise my own kids, outside the bustle of Hollywood.

My daughter saved my life. She came as a surprise but at a time when the warm glow of *Field of Dreams* was waning and I was back to playing roles that were less uplifting: those of rich jerks and fathers of abducted children. I played a series of them in the same way that I had suffered a string of ignominious deaths before *Field of Dreams* and the cumulative effect of the work darkened my worldview.

When I found out I was going to have a child, I secretly hoped it would be a girl, but my wife and I chose not to find out the sex of the baby in advance. I have always had great friendships with women and I told myself a girl would be easier to parent. When Lily was born, I was ecstatic.

I took a graphic video of the birth that NO ONE WILL EVER SEE but the camera may have distracted me sufficiently to keep me from passing out. I surprised myself with my eagerness to jump into the fatherhood I had so feared. I spent almost every morning alone with my daughter for her first few years so her mother could sleep in from doing the one part of parenting I couldn't do no matter how much I wanted to: breast-feeding.

Instead, I changed a lot of diapers and, like a real man, I developed some serious skill and perfected a few of my own systems to expedite the process. I became like a calf roper at the rodeo, sometimes throwing my hands over my head after changing a diaper in record time. It became my "area of expertise."

I was fascinated by everything that came out of her mouth as well. There was something about her perfect innocence and the amazing dawning of knowledge that was endlessly fascinating to me. I particularly loved our commute to pre-school.

One morning, as we drove through a drizzling rain, I turned to see her in her car seat staring at the windshield wipers, crying softly. "What's wrong, honey?" I asked, eager to fix any problem she was having.

With tears running down her cheeks from her enormous brown eyes, she said in a mournful voice I had never heard before, "The rain doesn't know who I am ..."

When my wife was finally ready to have another baby five years later, I wanted a son. I was still worried about the future conflicts that I was convinced were inherent in the father-son dynamic, but having had some amazing experiences with my daughter, I felt ready for the challenge.

Woodrow couldn't have been more different from his sister. He was shy and cautious and it felt like he spent the entire first few years of his life on my back, peeking out from behind my head. It was fun to see the world from his point of view, while feeling him breathing in my ear and wriggling in his backpack. He was born near my birthday and we are alike in many ways. He is a quiet dreamer like I am and we have always had an easy rapport. Now that he is a teenager, however, I think I am harder on my son than I was on my daughter.

With Woody, I worry more about his ability to someday provide for a family, a responsibility I haven't always felt I shouldered well myself. I want for him to have all the qualities I like best about myself: politeness, a sense of humor, a capacity for hard work, curiosity, a good ear for listening, and a genuine love of people. But I flinch when I see in him the qualities I dislike in myself: distractability, fear of conflict, timidity and a lack of confidence.

When the ball got pitched to him in his flag football games, I cringed to watch the familiar panic in his eyes from the pressure of the opponent's sudden attention and the expectation of the gathered parents that he should do something spectacular. All of the coaching to "Relax," and "Have fun," are meaningless sometimes when it feels like the eyes of the world are on you. Some boys are made for that kind of spotlight; others are not.

Despite his shyness, Woody is clever and funny and he asks a lot of questions. When he made up stories as a child, he would get so excited and talk so fast that I couldn't interrupt to ask a question, frequently punctuating the story with "Dad," as if to make sure I was listening, even when I was looking right at him. "Hey, Dad, there was this penguin with a jet pack, Dad, and he was a superhero, Dad, and he could fly and, hey Dad ..."

Parenting, unlike baseball, is an activity where your progress is not marked by a scoring system. By the time you figure out you're making a mistake, it feels like it's too late to do anything about it.

Despite wanting to be different than my dad, I keep telling myself that who my father was helped make me who I am. It is easy to end up in a circular pursuit to be the dad we wanted, while our children just need us to be the dads we are. For all my other mistakes as a father, with my children I make sure there are no shortages of hugs or "I love you's."

Another unexpected upside of having been in a mediocre film like *The Guardian*, was that its theatrical release, in May of 1990, coincided with the VHS release of a classic American film, *Harvey*. Since both films were Universal pictures, I received a call from the head of publicity at the studio, a lovely woman named Jane Ayer, who asked me if I would like to come to a promotional event at a Blockbuster video store in Marina del Rey, close to my Venice apartment.

Jane had always been very generous and kind to me during the release of *Field of Dreams*, whenever I asked her for t-shirts or posters to donate for local charity fundraisers. We shared a love of classic old movies and loved to talk about our favorite old-time movie stars.

When I arrived at the video store on Lincoln Boulevard, there was already a line forming out the front door. As I made my way to the back door, as I'd been instructed, workers were putting the finishing touches on the backdrop of movie posters for the press to take pictures in front of. I could see Jane talking animatedly to a tall, older man in a blue blazer whose back was to me.

As I walked up to talk to Jane, the man turned toward me and I found myself looking into an oddly familiar face.

"Mr. Stewart, I'd like you to meet Dwier Brown. He's in a Universal movie that's opening next week. Dwier, this is Jimmy Stewart."

He held his hand out to me and I shook it. I'm not sure if my mouth was hanging open, but it felt like it was. All I could think about was how tall he was but how small his hand felt in mine. "It's nice to finally meet you, Mr. Stewart. I'm a big fan of your movies."

"Thank you. I-It-It's a pleasure to meet you." *He stuttered his words! Just like he did in his movies! Just like I did when I tried to impersonate him in front of the bathroom mirror when I was a kid!* I was finally face-to-face with Jimmy Stewart and I couldn't believe it.

He must have been accustomed to people staring at him with their mouths open, because Jane continued their conversation and he turned his attention back to her without excluding me from their discussion. I stood there, listening and nodding absently to their dialogue, like a six-foot tall invisible rabbit.

Is This Heaven?

*"No matter what it is a writer is writing about, if the writer is a man,
he is writing about the search for his father."*

– William Faulkner

One Halloween afternoon, a few years after my father died, I stopped at a mall in North Hollywood to get a bandana for a pirate costume I planned to wear that night. I entered on the upper level and walked to the railing at the center of the mall to find the store I was looking for. When I looked down to the lower level, I noticed that the mall was filled with children in costumes, walking with their parents.

An unseen force squeezed my chest and a tingling sensation erupted behind my eyes. Tears started pouring out of my eyes and I doubled over, sobbing violently.

I was embarrassed to be crying on a fake leather bench in a busy mall, but my pain had taken control and, like a vomiting reflex, it racked my body in wave after wave, until finally the tears passed like a summer cloudburst, leaving me clean as a steaming sidewalk.

Why the loss of my father finally hit me on that day, in that way, I still don't know.

I peeled my sticky face off of the shiny, vinyl bench and looked around at the bustle of children and parents, who seemed oblivious to my sudden grief. Then I slowly got to my feet and walked to my car.

I sometimes feel cheated that my dad only lived 67 years until I hear someone else's story about their father's death at 60 or 55 or 49. They would give anything for a few more years. I would, too. But unlike many fathers and sons whose tearful stories have been told to me, at least he *knew* I loved him and I knew he loved me.

Communicating such a thing was difficult in my dad's generation. In the era of *Father Knows Best* and moms as full-time homemakers, it was more difficult to forge a meaningful relationship with a guy who spent a third of his life at his workplace and another third mildly exhausted. Maybe it's easier now, in our age of shared parental responsibility and more fathers that are encouraged to spend quality time with their children. I imagine my father would have enjoyed being a stay-at-home dad, if such a thing had been more acceptable in his time.

I had pried some stories out of him that helped me get to know who he really was. It hadn't been easy. Men aren't chatty about such things, particularly the things that have hurt them. My father had grown up knowing that any revealing comments he made might be used against his mother and siblings in his father's quest for a divorce. He had built a house of secrets as a boy and, as a man, sometimes couldn't find his way out of it.

My father took early retirement when he was 62. His employer in Akron, Firestone Tire, was offering early retirement packages to its senior employees and Dad had been there 23 years. He looked at it like an insurance actuary might. I remember him telling me, "The average life expectancy for men is 67 years. If I take my retirement at 65, I won't have much time to enjoy it."

He ended up with five years and I think he did enjoy them. He painted, he built intricate wood models of the U.S.S. Constitution and the Mayflower and he took my mother to Hawaii and Europe and to Chicago to visit me. He wrote me the one and only letter I ever received from him, and it rambled mostly about a squirrel that was confounding his every effort to protect his precious birdfeeders. It is one of my cherished possessions.

In the end, I think my father was ready to die. He had redeemed his father's abandonment of him and showed his father how a man should take care of his children. With his work done and his kids far away, my father's dream of early retirement was a hollow reward. He had nothing left to do and no one left to depend on him. He died like his pension actuarial chart had predicted for an "average American male," on schedule at 67.

When the weight of my father's death finally hit me, I wanted the world to stop for a few minutes to acknowledge his passing. It felt like my world had changed in some profound way and I wanted there to be some reflection of it in the greater world around me. I don't know what I expected, but it felt like businesses should close for a week out of respect, so that everyone could have some time to adjust to the loss. Of course, this was not the case. Life is nothing if not relentless.

The simplest actions, like buying toothpaste in a drugstore, felt strange and false. I expected strangers to know by looking at me that something terrible had happened and to silently embrace me. When they didn't acknowledge my diminished world, I felt even more alienated, like some cruel universal hoax was being played on me.

I was, of course, aware that my father had not made the earth-shattering discoveries or life-changing contributions necessary for his death to be headline news. But I also knew that he had suffered the pain of his father's coldness and forced himself to be the kind of father he had wanted for himself. The depth of that small but profound effort seemed worthy of the fanfare usually reserved for the mighty and I wanted that for him.

Life goes on, even if sometimes you don't want it to. After my father's death and the excitement of *Field of Dreams* and the disappointment of my next movies by comparison, slowly, one small effort at a time, I made my way back to my life. The banalities of existence gradually absorbed the thoughts about the loss of my father. They were replaced with occasional unexpected feelings that he was near me, in random places, while I was walking in a park or reading in a chair on the patio.

I would feel him behind me and stop what I was doing, only to have the feeling disappear as quickly as it had come. Despite the brevity of these encounters, they were comforting to me.

One night, as I walked up the meandering series of 75 rustic steps I had built from the creek to my fixer-upper house, a strong breeze blew up out of nowhere, so suddenly that it got my attention. I paused on the steps for a moment and looked at the feathery elm trees tossing wildly in the wind and wondered what had caused this sudden sustained gust of warm air. I was overwhelmed with the feeling of my father's presence again and I stood still with the wind blowing fiercely around me.

I do not believe in ghosts, but I felt very clearly that my father was communicating to me in some way through that unusual breeze. Like in a dream, I "knew" somehow it was my father, even though his presence was lighter, happier, more excited than I had ever remembered him. I stood still on that step with the pepper tree leaves spiraling into the air around me and "listened" to my father.

I did not hear his voice, but I absorbed his message as if hearing the words of a distant song. He told me that it was time for him to move on. He had been waiting and watching me and he now felt like I was happy in my new home with my magical little creek and that it was time for him to go. He had other things to do.

I don't know how long I stood on that step, but I waited as the wind buffeted my body and tossed the trees and I leaned gently into its gusts to keep my balance. I reached to understand what was happening to me and to make sure I had heard everything he wanted to say. When the breeze abruptly died down, the air felt light and clear. There was nothing more.

A few days after my father's death in 1988, as I walked alone around the yard of our old farm, I saw the beautiful chunk of pink granite at the end of the driveway. I sat on it, looked down, and watched the sunlight sparkle off the facets of crystal and mica imbedded in the stone.

I remembered my father's quiet determination to remove this stubborn boulder from his dream basement, the sweat he had shed to accomplish the feat, and the triumph he felt when we placed it as a sentry at the end of the driveway.

The huge rock looked happy there, as if its implacable nature had somehow wordlessly challenged my father to wrestle it from the cold ground and out of the dark basement where it could shed its layers of dirt and finally feel the wind and glisten in the sun.

By the time I went back inside, I had hatched an idea and I shared it with my family. Why not use this chunk of granite, a symbol of Dad's life's work of remodeling our house, as the guardian of his final resting place? This was a monument that he had touched and cursed and wrestled with his own hands, one that had tested his stoic determination, one that had drawn blood, but one that had been conquered.

Everyone agreed that the rock would be a fitting headstone. I found a company that did rock etching and they assured that they could move the stone and sandblast the appropriate words onto the rough surface.

Even with their heavy-duty winch and boom, they had trouble getting the rock onto their flatbed truck. I knew Dad would have wanted to be there helping them.

I showed them where we wanted the epitaph placed and they secured the massive pink rock onto their truck and took it for its first drive.

A few weeks later, the large rock was lowered onto its final resting place above my father's grave.

Lying in a handsome, walnut casket, under six feet of dirt and a massive, rough chunk of radiant pink granite, lies my father, "Walter Warren Brown, 1921-1988." A humble epitaph for a humble man, but a hero to a few of us, at least.

In the two-and-a-half decades since *Field of Dreams* was released in 1989, dozens of people have come up to me to tell me how seeing the movie has affected their lives and to share a story about their father or their daughter or their son. I try to absorb every word and soak up every nuance, as if it were my father talking to me again about important things, the things that hurt him and the things that made him happy.

Because most fathers can't talk about the important things. It is only the wordless activities you are engaged in, like playing catch or working, that indicate that it *is* meaningful.

It has been a gift to have had my face endowed by the movie with a free pass to people's most tender feelings. My appearance comes at a time in the film when the rest of the cast and crew have done the hard labor to open the audience's heart, and all I have to do is take off my catcher's mask and walk right in.

Maybe there was something about my taking the catcher's mask off at the end of the film, about a catcher taking off his protective gear. Maybe it invites others to take off their protective gear and talk about the things they aren't usually allowed to talk about, for fear of getting hurt.

It has been said that playing catch is a powerful activity for men, because it is a silent ritual that mimics what we have such difficulty doing, particularly with our fathers, our sons and our daughters. Throwing the ball is like saying "I give to you" and catching it is like saying "I get from you."

"I give to you, I get from you."

"I give to you, I get from you," over and over again.

ABOUT THE AUTHOR

Dwier Brown has been a professional actor for 35 years and has performed in over a hundred movies and plays and on television shows such as *House M.D., CSI, Firefly, the Thorn Birds, ER* and *Ally McBeal.* He is perhaps best known for playing Kevin Costner's father as a young man in *Field of Dreams.* Mr. Brown has co-founded three theatre companies as well as the Ojai Playwrights Conference. *If You Build It...* is his first book. He lives in Ojai, California with his wife and children and their dog, Grandma.

ACKNOWLEDGEMENTS

"It is impossible to be judgmental and grateful at the same time."
-Gary Douglas and Dr. Dain Heer

My wife Laurie is the light of my life. She is a walking, talking, dancing, singing, sexy vaudeville show that I was lucky enough to marry. She persevered through my leaving our warm, delicious bed at 3 a.m. to write every night (in truth, she "forced" me to do it, because I can't concentrate on anything else when she's awake), and supported me endlessly by designing a website and the book cover and promoting my efforts in a hundred different ways. She soothed my rants of waning self-confidence and somehow ignored my escalating curses at the computer.

My children Lily and Woodrow have endured my bleary gaze, short attention span and frequent midday naps while I (ironically) wrote a book about being a good father. Our solution to facebook is called realface*, and it involves the novel idea of communicating with someone else without the use of a computer. (*patent pending). My children save my life and bring me joy daily.

Our amazing dog, Grandma, offered me perfect, deadpan stares to dampen any pretension that my writing a book could possibly be more important than escorting her around the neighborhood to pee.

I waited a long time to send a copy of the finished manuscript to my mother in Ohio, because I felt guilty that she was not featured more prominently in it. But the truth is, I didn't write more about my mother because she has always been a steady, positive force in my life and I never felt a struggle to "know" her the way I did for many years with my father.

My mother was a movie fan as a girl and always gave unflinching support to our many theatrical exploits, from sewing puppets for our basement puppet shows to doing a cameo in our Busby Berkeley spoof, *Tarnished Tinsel*, when we were teenagers.

She has always been my biggest fan and she has harangued many of her friends and fellow church members into witnessing my various deaths on television (many thanks to my North Canton fan club: Yvonne Hawley, Allyn and Gaylen Colbert, Elsie Brooks, Gini Spring, Sue Child and Holly and Jeanne Brownewell).

Mom has always been a voracious reader and my love of writing letters and my desire to one day write a book came from her. That is not to say she didn't have a half dozen grammatical notes for me once she read it. I love you, Mom.

I started writing this book two and a half years ago and I brought my five or six pages a week to a writing group, the Wednesday Morning Dilletantes, or "WMD's" for short. Over the years, some of our six members have come and gone, but I couldn't have written this book without their weekly support and criticism, and the inspiration of hearing their writing week after week. Kathleen Rainey, Brad David, James Lashly, Christy Sebastian, and Chris Westphal have all done more to shape this book than they know, and without whose unflagging support, I could not have persevered the brutal onslaughts of my own inner critic.

Leading this group was a brilliant spark of light named Deb Norton. Her laser insights and unsinkable optimism saved me many times from despair and surrender. She supported us all and found ways to keep us writing through many a dark moment and even allowed me to work around her house in exchange for staying in the group when I couldn't afford it.

Alas, she moved away so she could finish her own book about writing and keeping one's inner critic at bay, which I highly recommend you read as soon as it is available. In the meantime, introduce yourself to her wisdom and her unflaggable spirit with her blog posts on www.partwild.com.

Taking over our group when Deb left was her cosmic writing twin, Elizabeth Schwyzer, who continues to push us buoyantly to our best writing and gave me valuable, frank editorial notes that have helped immeasurably in the final stages of writing this book. Check out www.lizzywrites.com

The adventure of writing a book about the crazy, synchronistic world of my *Field of Dreams* experience would not be complete without a few "meant-to-be moments."

My high school buddy, Mark Kuhar, who first gave me the book *Shoeless Joe* back in 1986, was the first one to read my sprawling mess of a manuscript and offer me valuable "outside" feedback and editorial advice. His opinion as a long-time editor, poet and friend were crucial to my process.

Lawrence Kessenich is the man who convinced W.P. Kinsella to expand his 25-page short story into the novel *Shoeless Joe*, from which *Field of Dreams* was made. For him to agree to edit this book for me was a coup and truly brought the process full circle. Lawrence's astute judgment provided just the right sensibilities to the book when it needed it most. His second volume of poetry is about to be published and will be available on amazon.

Brian Frankish, the executive producer of the film (he also played the umpire), offered great stories and corroboration of circumstances and events that, as an actor, I was only peripherally aware of. As Brian says, "I think we all made that movie for our fathers," and "it's still the best thing on my resume'." I think a lot of us involved with the film feel the same way.

Many thanks to Jane Ayer, whose kindness to me when she worked at Universal Studios in 1989 was almost unbounded, and her enthusiasm for and assistance with this book was a great inspiration to me. She single-handedly made my dream of meeting Jimmy Stewart come true. As a tribute to her quiet charm, her name has now been mentioned in at least five books, from David Rensin's book about surfer icon Miki Dora to two memoirs from rock legends Led Zeppelin.

I would like to thank Don and Becky Lansing, who answered my questions and re-introduced me to the beautiful ballfield in Dyersville. They provided photos, support, stories, a load of laughs and the hospitality of their beautiful home. Don's sister Betty Boeckenstedt has collected extensive notes and demographic information about the million visitors who have come to the field over the years, which she delivered to me with her incredible smile. 85 year-old Annie Vaske, who was Don's first employee is a feisty, charming keeper of stories about the early visitors to the field.

Perusing the scores of guest registers and reading the touching and funny entries by fans of the film was an endless source of amusement. Among my favorite entries:

"No hot dogs after one choking incident??? C'mon!"

"We would have spent more time and dollars here, but the goddam highway patrol just wrote us up a speeding ticket."

Overwhelmingly, the entries thank the Lansings for "keeping the dream alive" and for taking care of the field. Also reflected many times in the guestbook entries is gratitude for "no admission charge." Don is 72 and still putters around the movie site daily. Say "hi" to him for me if he suddenly pops up next to you at the field.

My journey to my acting career was aided immeasurably by Hildagarde Bender, Murray Hudson, Jim Reynolds, Edward Kaye-Martin, Joanne Baron and Kim Maxwell.

My friend David Feigin offered me a sympathic ear, sage advice and consistent encouragement while he ran me, cursing, around a baseball diamond.

Many writing binges were rewarded with delicious meals provided by Jeff and Kasey, the generous owners of Papa Lennon's Pizzeria in Ojai, California.

I would like to thank Evan Fong, Dave Fulton, Melinda Sue Gordon, Deidre Theiman, Jessica Taylor, and Roni Lubliner, Margery Simkin, Stacey Behlmer and Warren Sherk (at the Academy of Motion Picture Arts and Sciences' Margaret Herrick Library), Sue Reidel, Ty Ballou, Brian Koeberle, John Anderson, Gary Frontier, Paulette Mahurin, David Rensin, Scott Clements and Brad Herzog at WhyNotBooks.com. Special thanks to David Reeser and Amy Schneider at OjaiDigital.com.

Of course, this book would not have been possible without Bill Kinsella's wonderful novel *Shoeless Joe*. Or without Phil Alden Robinson's brilliant adaptation and direction of *Field of Dreams*. Or Larry and Chuck Gordon's perseverance in getting it made, Kevin Costner's willingness to sign on to it, Tom Pollock's greenlighting of it finally at Universal and on and on. In particular, I will never be able to sufficiently thank Phil for his selection of me for this small role that has meant so much to me and his kindness and generosity with me ever since.

Lastly, I would like to thank all of you who have approached me over the years to tell me how *Field of Dreams* changed your lives. It was your stories that first inspired me to write this book. If your story was one of dozens that didn't make it into this book, I apologize, but know that your story is still filed in my head and may make it into another book, God willing.

The movie *Field of Dreams* was instrumental in helping me realize many of my lifelong dreams. It answered my prayers of being in a movie that was meaningful to people and created the added bonus of continually sending those people into my path to tell me about it. The film managed to get me into one of the Top 100 Movie Moments of all time, the Baseball Hall of Fame and gave me the opportunity to meet my idol, Jimmy Stewart. Now it has given me the reason to write this book. That's not a bad legacy for five minutes of screen time.

THANK YOU

Al & Rita Ameskamp

Lt. Commander Terry Alvord

Richard Arrington

John Augustine

Ty Ballou

Ryan Ballou

Ryder Ballou

Bill Barnes

Bruce Barnes

For my father, Harold Barsema

Dave & Gina Bauer

Tricia Behnke

Earl Bender

Maxwell Lewis Bible I, II & III

Evie June Lula Bible

Jim & Betty Boeckenstedt

Don Bonezzi

1st Lt. Clarence E. Boyle, Jr.

Evelyn Brooks

Stella Wood Dwier Brown

Edward Irving Brown III

Edward Irving Brown IV

Edward Irving Brown V

William George Brown

Walter Warren Brown

Elsie Jean Ferris Brown

Barbara Winifred Brown

Steve Brownewell

Patty Burns-Coley

Richard Chaffee

Robert Chaffee

Rick Cleveland

Allyn Colbert

Gaylen Colbert

James & Lorna Tuck Colbert

Peter & Paul Colbert

Nancy Conley

Jane DeVries Cooper

Keith Crockett

Mary Cunningham

George & Carol Davis

Rod Dedeaux

Faron Drosnos

Richard Feightner

Martin Feigin

Selma Rubenstein Feigin Sherman

Fred E. Ferris

Jessie Margaret Porter Ferris

Janiece Fisher

Gary Fonville

Jack Frankish

Rev. Doug Garwood

Stephen Garwood

George Gordon

Dr. Pedro Guinto

Cindy Heacock

Patti McCollum Higgins

Curtis Hood

Jim Hunton

Cal Kalicki

Virg Kass

Edward Kaye-Martin

Bob Keck

Bill & Ruth Kelly

Jim & Gail Kelly

Ben Kelly

Jennifer & Pete Klatka

Abby & Lucy Klatka

Tom & Cynthia Klimasz

Dr. Marko Kuhar

LaVern & Bernice Lansing

Don & Becky Lansing

Ruth Lansing

Mike Leatherberry

Debbie Urbach Lennon

Kipp & Jody Lennon Family

William & Isabelle Lennon

Ted & Peggy Lennon

Thomas Patrick Lennon

Shawn Lippincott

Doug & Beth Mann

Kristin Mann

Alex Mann

Maria Mann

Ed & Lynn Mann

Katie Stephenson & Steve May

Chloe May

Randy McVay

Caitriona Meek

Dave Miller

Alan Nicholson

Elizabeth & Nick Nolan

Izzi Nolan

Mark & Barbara Nolind

Becky Norton

Barack & Michelle Obama

Nate Orchard

Bob & Beth Pacanowski

Gene Payne

Cathy & Bill Pratscher

Cindy Pribish

Chris Riehm

Coach Rinehart

Arland Rininger

Robert Ritcher

Robert Ritcher, Jr.

S. JESSE & JESSIE ROBINSON

GEORGE & BETTY ROGERS

SHIRLEY SAVAGE

SERGEANT KARL SEITER

BILL SEXAUER

TOM SEXAUER

LINDA SNYDER SHANDLE

KEVIN SHAW

DOUGLAS FREDERICK SPRINGSTEEN

MARYLOU THOMAS

VAL ULRICH

BUTCH & ANNIE VASKE

JERRY VORNDRAN

JIM VORNDRAN

JOHN VORNDRAN

WENDY WASSER

MARCIA WEIGEL

DAVID & DOLORES WIATROSKI

DOUG WISE

DIANE ZEILE

"And I know a father
Who had a son
He longed to tell him all the reasons
For the things he'd done
He came a long way
Just to explain
He kissed his boy as he lay sleeping
Then he turned around and headed home again"

- Paul Simon, *Slip Sliding Away*

If you enjoyed this book,
please help me spread the word with
a rating or review on:

Amazon.com
and
GoodReads.com

It only takes a minute and it would make my day!

Thanks,

CPSIA information can be obtained at www.ICGtesting.com
Printed in the USA
BVOW05s1520040615

403029BV00003B/141/P